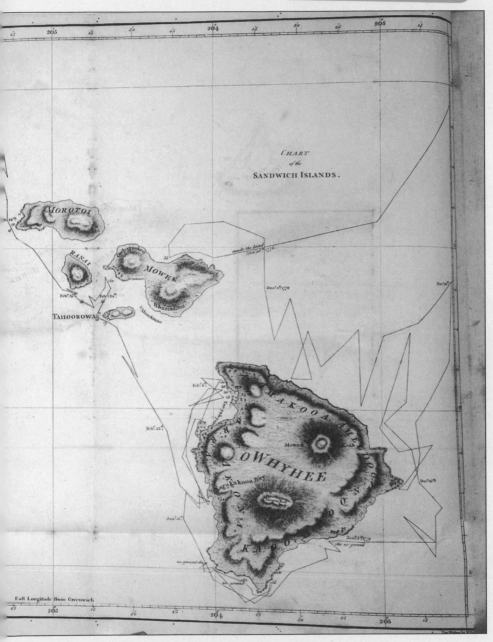

CHART
of the
SANDWICH ISLANDS.

East Longitude from Greenwich

THE DEATH OF CAPTAIN COOK

THE DEATH OF CAPTAIN COOK

A HERO MADE AND UNMADE

GLYN WILLIAMS

Harvard University Press
Cambridge, Massachusetts
2008

Printed in the United States of America

First published in the United Kingdom
by Profile Books, Ltd.
3A Exmouth House
Pine Street
London EC1R OJH

Library of Congress Cataloging-in-Publication Data

Williams, Glyndwr.
The death of Captain Cook : a hero made and unmade / Glyn Williams.
p. cm
Includes index.
ISBN 978-0-674-03194-4 (alk. paper)
1. Cook, James, 1728–1779—Travel.   2. Cook, James, 1728–1779—Death
and burial.   3. Explorers—Great Britain—Biography.   I. Title.
G246.C7W47   2008
910.92—dc22 [B] 2008008827

For Alan
scholar, poet, friend

CONTENTS

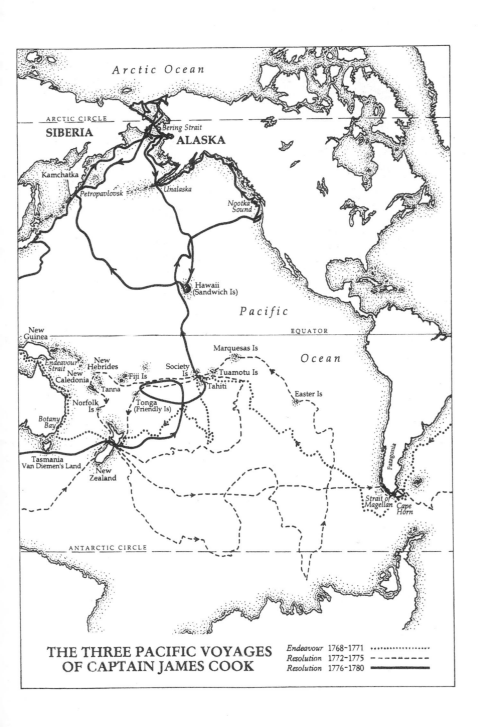

THE THREE PACIFIC VOYAGES
OF CAPTAIN JAMES COOK

Endeavour 1768–1771 ....
Resolution 1772–1775 – – – – – – – –
Resolution 1776–1780 ▬▬▬▬▬▬

1. *A classical hero, the marble bust of Captain Cook by Lucien Le Vieux, 1790, based on Augustin Pajou's sculpture for a monument commissioned by the Marquis de la Borde, a French admirer of Cook.*

INTRODUCTION

Captain Cook's enduring claim to fame is that he redrew the map of the world. In three extraordinary voyages he transformed Europe's sketchy and incomplete knowledge of the Pacific. Sailing many thousands of miles across the largely uncharted ocean that covered almost one-third of the earth's surface, he mapped lands from New Zealand in the south to Hawai'i in the north on a scale and in a detail no previous voyager had done. As one of his officers proudly remarked after the third voyage, 'The Grand bounds of the four Quarters of the Globe are known.' In addition to his skills in navigation and surveying, Cook possessed those less tangible qualities of leadership, determination and humanity, which made him the outstanding explorer of his time. For a man of humble origins and relatively junior rank there was something breathtaking about his stated ambition not only to go 'farther than any man has been before me, but as far as I think it possible for man to go', and in this he succeeded.

Compared with most of his predecessors in the age of European overseas expansion Cook was an unusual explorer, one devoted to the arts of peace, who furnished the Pacific islands with crops, implements and livestock, and (in the opinion of the then President of the Royal Society) never 'wantonly or unnecessarily' opened fire on their inhabitants.

The shipboard journals described Cook's skills in placating wary islanders in that perilous moment of landing from an open boat on an unknown coast; he was always first ashore, carrying no weapon, but with hands outstretched in a gesture of friendliness. He led, it seemed, a charmed life. The news that reached England in early 1780 that Cook had been killed on a beach in Hawai'i the previous February was therefore shocking and astonishing, and there was a tense period of waiting until the ships returned home with more details of Cook's final voyage.

The first reports about the events leading to Cook's death were far from reassuring. There were rumours that he had been treated as a god, Lono, by the Hawaiians, and had accepted their adoration. Attempts by the Admiralty at prohibition and censorship failed when unofficial accounts were published, but their sensational testimonies were overborne when the authorised account of the voyage appeared. This weighty publication acknowledged the Lono issue, but presented the tangled sequence of Cook's last hours as the moving story of a leader who gave his life to save others. Evidence to the contrary was ignored, and the mysterious disappearance – never explained – of the last, crucial section of Cook's own journal allowed an editor in England a free hand to shape and polish the published account. In this, little was made of Cook's worrying outbursts of violence on the voyage, or of the concern of some of his officers about his behaviour shortly before his death. 'His humanity proved fatal to him' was the explanation that confirmed the emergence of a new and saintly hero to a public looking for reassurance after the disastrous American war.

My interpretation of Cook breaks new ground as I argue that the circumstances and reporting of his death are the key to his reputation. The turning of his impetuous behaviour in the bloody and chaotic fracas on the beach at Kealakekua Bay into something altogether nobler and more sacrificial became the defining moment – captured in words and pictures – in the establishment of a martyr-hero. Official and unofficial records, newspapers and periodicals show that only after his death was there widespread appreciation of Cook's achievements. Posthumous tributes made much of his qualities as a navigator and hydrographer, his care for the health of his crews, and his humane dealings with the different peoples he encountered on his voyages. He was more famous dead than alive, but while many celebrated Cook as the man who brought European values to the Pacific, others suspected that it would have been better if 'the South Seas had still remained unknown to Europe and its restless inhabitants'. This dualism runs through the rest of the book.

For decades after his death, Cook enjoyed a status as 'a mariner and discoverer, incomparable and unique, the pride of his century'. The words are those of George Forster, the scholarly young foreigner who sailed on the second voyage, and are a reminder that the books, charts and views from Cook's voyages came off the presses, not only in Britain, but in France, Holland, Germany, Russia and Italy as well. Cook became a figure of European renown, and the site of his death at Kealakekua Bay was visited as a place of pilgrimage by seamen of all nations. In much of Polynesia, Cook was venerated as a powerful ancestral chief from distant parts, while in the Pacific colonies of white settlement he became 'father of the nation', whose merits as a self-made man seemed to reflect the pioneering spirit of Australians, New Zealanders and British Columbians.

By contrast, in Hawai'i a different interpretation of Cook

emerged, one in which his death was a fitting punishment for an idolater and a libertine. In recent years this view has found a ready response in the postcolonial world. More than two hundred years after the event an explosive interplay between academic scholarship and local feelings has centred on the death of Cook. In some parts of the world today 'Captain Cook' is as much iconic invader as torch-bearer of the Enlightenment, as much anti-hero as hero. His progress from obscurity to fame, and then for some, to infamy, is a story that has never been fully told.

1

A DISTANT DEATH

POOR CAPTAIN COOKE IS NO MORE

On Friday, 12 July 1776, Captain Cook left Plymouth Sound on his third Pacific voyage of discovery. Sailing in the *Resolution*, the Whitby-built collier that had performed stoutly on his second voyage, he hoped to find the entrance of the Northwest Passage, the link between the Atlantic and Pacific Oceans that had been sought by Europe's seamen for almost three centuries. The newspapers of the day made little of Cook's departure. The layout of the broadsheets, with their packed pages and small print, did not allow for headlines, and in any case more portentous matters were afoot. In the American colonies hostilities had broken out at Bunker Hill a year earlier, and a few days before Cook sailed the Declaration of American Independence had been signed in Philadelphia.

More immediate worries bothered Cook. The *Resolution*'s hull had been so poorly caulked in the Deptford shipyards that her First Lieutenant, John Gore, complained that if he survived the voyage 'the next Trip I may Safely Venture in a Ship Built of Ginger Bread'. Of more concern still was the fact that the consort vessel, the *Discovery*, was left behind because her captain, the convivial and high-spirited Charles Clerke, veteran of three Pacific voyages, was held in London as surety for his brother's debts, and was three weeks late joining Cook at the Cape of Good Hope. The delay put Cook well behind schedule, and there was a touch of irritation in his letter from the Cape to the Earl of Sandwich, First Lord of the Admiralty, on 26 November; 'We are at length ready to put to sea and proceed on the voyage.' On 1 December 1776 the two ships headed out of Table Bay, and passed out of sight. There would be no further news of them for more than three years.

Cook was, in Sandwich's words to the House of Lords, 'the first navigator in Europe'. On his first Pacific voyage in the *Endeavour* Lieutenant Cook (as he then was) had put more than 5,000 miles of previously unknown coastline on the map. After a stay at Tahiti to observe the transit of Venus he had charted the twin islands of New Zealand, the east coast of Australia, and Torres Strait. This feat of sustained exploration had been accomplished without the loss of a single man from scurvy, that scourge of long ocean voyages, although in cruel contrast almost a third of the crew died from land-borne diseases picked up at Java on the homeward voyage. Within a year of his return to England, Cook was at sea again. His second Pacific expedition was one of the most comprehensive of all voyages of discovery. In his three years away he disposed of the imagined southern continent, reached closer to the South Pole than any man before, and touched on a multitude of lands – Tahiti and New Zealand again, and for the first time Easter Island, the Marquesas, Tonga, New Caledonia and the New Hebrides (Vanuatu). In two voyages he had drawn the modern map of the South Pacific.

After his two long and strenuous voyages there was at first no inclination at the Admiralty to ask Cook to return to the Pacific, but gradually he was drawn into the planning process for what was to be his third voyage. Cook's first biographer, Andrew Kippis, describes how Sandwich and his colleagues at the Admiralty were reluctant to ask Cook to serve again, but in February 1776 arranged a dinner party to discuss the practical details of the forthcoming voyage. After animated discussion of the grand design to find the Northwest Passage, Kippis relates, 'Captain Cook was so fired with the contemplation and representation of the object, that he started up, and declared that he himself would undertake the direction of the enterprise.' Biographers must be allowed their moments of drama, but the fact was that Cook needed little persuasion. When appointed to a comfortable retirement post at Greenwich Hospital within a few days of arriving home from the Pacific in the summer of 1775, he had made it clear that he would gladly return to active service if the call came. Cook was forty-seven, but he wrote to John Walker, who had employed him when as a young man he was ship's master of a collier operating out of Whitby in Yorkshire, wondering whether 'I can bring my self to like ease and retirement', and suspecting that the limits of Greenwich Hospital 'are far too small for an active mind like mine'.

Had the proposed voyage been of a more routine nature, then Cook would probably not have been tempted; but the challenge of the Northwest Passage was different. It was as long-standing an objective of European maritime endeavour as the supposed southern continent, whose shadowy existence had dominated Cook's first two Pacific voyages. Moreover, with the fame and honour of a successful voyage would come a major share of the £20,000 parliamentary award for the first discoverer of the Passage. This may have been an important motive for one who did not possess any inherited wealth, but who was increasingly moving in circles of society well beyond the means of an ordinary naval officer. Four days after his appointment, Cook wrote again to John Walker telling him about the new voyage, and adding, 'If I am fortunate enough to get safe home, there is no doubt but it will be greatly to my advantage.' The last words suggest some quiet commitments and pledges by those in authority.

With hindsight, knowing the fatal outcome of the voyage, we can argue that Cook should not have been approached, not had the great prize dangled before him. For all but one of the previous seven years he had been away on voyages that were physically gruelling and mentally exhausting. If he had remained in the Whitby coal trade he would almost certainly have retired by this time, for the masters of colliers 'felt themselves hard done by when their aching limbs were still at sea at the age of 40'. As he sailed into uncharted waters and reached unknown lands and their peoples, he alone had taken all decisions. At no time was there a superior at hand to give counsel and support. During those years the sturdy physique and self-reliant disposition of the tall Yorkshireman had borne the strain, but on his second voyage he had twice been ill, on the latter occasion dangerously so. In the North Pacific he would be faced with new problems and dangers. They were met resolutely, and mostly overcome, but at a cost to Cook's judgement that in the end resulted in violence and death.

As the ships reached the Pacific the timetable for the voyage continued to slip, and Cook's patience ran out. Among the islands floggings, cropping of ears, burnings of huts and canoes, reflected his exasperation. Sailors as well as Polynesians felt the weight of Cook's anger; forty-four of the *Resolution*'s crew were flogged compared to nineteen on the second voyage, a total of 604 lashes as against 288. The turning-point of the voyage came in the summer of 1778 on the Alaskan coast when Cook, already a season later than planned, was driven to distraction by his failure to find a passage. Venturing into unfamiliar Arctic waters, he relied too heavily on untrustworthy Russian maps, and wasted hours and energy that could be ill afforded. For the first time on his Pacific voyages Cook was haunted by the continual worry of all Arctic explorers, the shortness of the navigable season. Time and again he was faced with deciding whether he should leave inlets and stretches of coastline unexplored in his haste to get north, or stay to investigate at the cost of arriving at a passage too late in the season. In a letter written to the Admiralty in October 1778 and entrusted to Russian traders in Unalaska, Cook admitted:

> We were upon a Coast ... where no information could be had from Maps, either modern or ancient: confiding too much in the former we were frequently misled to our no small hindrance.

Cook's survey of the northwest coast of America was a major achievement, but for him it had ended in failure.

From Unalaska the ships sailed 3,000 miles south to the Hawaiian Islands, a previously unknown group whose western outliers they had unexpectedly come across as they sailed over the North Pacific towards the American coast at the beginning of the year. Equally unexpected was the discovery that the islanders seemed to be of the same 'nation' as the people of Tahiti, Tonga and New Zealand in the South Pacific. This was more than a matter of academic interest, for the Hawaiians spoke the same (Polynesian) 'dialect' with which many of the crews were familiar. The ships reached the eastern islands of the archipelago in late November, but did not find harbour until mid-January. These final six weeks of frustration, with reduced allowances, angered the crew, longing for the fresh provisions and sexual comforts of the nearby shore. Some of them sent their captain 'a very mutinous letter', while Cook for his part stopped the crew's grog allowance, and wrote diatribes in his journal in which his 'mutinous turbulent crew' was condemned at one moment and the penny-pinching Admiralty the next. By the time the ships reached Kealakekua Bay on the southwest coast of the 'big island' of Hawai'i in January 1779, Cook was a weary, disappointed, and possibly quite sick man. Adding to the general depression that seemed to have overtaken the expedition was the death from tuberculosis in August 1778 of William Anderson, the talented young surgeon and naturalist of the *Endeavour* for whom, Cook wrote, he had 'a very high regard', and the knowledge that Captain Clerke was terminally ill from the same disease.

None of this was known in England. No eighteenth-century voyage of discovery had disappeared so completely from view for so long a period of time. On Cook's second voyage he had been out of touch with London for a little over two years, from April 1773 to June 1775. On his third voyage Cook planned to reach the northwest coast of America in the summer of 1777; whether he had found a passage there or not, it was difficult to understand why no news had been received from him for three years. Admiralty worries must have been sharpened by a letter from Sir James Harris, British Ambassador to the Russian court at St Petersburg. In November 1779 he forwarded to London a Russian report received from the remotest part of the Russian empire in Kamchatka, which described how in the autumn of 1777 two mysterious ships had appeared off the Aleutian Islands, whose crews, according to the islanders, dressed like Russians but did not speak Russian. The news was the first indication that Cook had reached the North Pacific, but it did more to alarm than reassure, for Harris's (mistaken) belief that the sighting had been made in 1777, not 1778, raised worrying questions about what had happened to the ships in the two years since.

As Harris made further investigations he saw another dispatch from Kamchatka that 'flung a dump on my enquirys, which were indeed become useless'. The package contained Cook's report written at Unalaska in October 1778, describing the voyage to that date. More poignantly, it also included a later letter from Captain Clerke, written in June 1779, with the shocking news that in February Cook had been killed on the island of 'Owhyee' (Hawai'i). Clerke's letter crossed Russia and reached London on 10 January 1780, accompanied by a note from Gore notifying the Admiralty that Clerke had since died from a 'lingering consumption', and that he was now in command of the expedition. In his letter Clerke recounted the extraordinary events of the previous winter: the landing at Kealakekua Bay on Hawai'i, the crews' rapturous reception by the islanders, 'whose benevolence and friendship exceeded every thing we had ever before met with', the ships' departure, and the unfortunate forced return when the Resolution's foremast was damaged. During the second stay at Kealakekua Bay a growing number of thefts irritated and angered Cook, and on the night of 13 February 1779 the Discovery's cutter was stolen. Clerke's description of events the next morning as Cook landed in an attempt to recover

the boat was the first, and for long the fullest, account of the
death of Cook to be received in England:

In the morning at day-light I waited upon Captain Cook
and acquainted him with it [the theft of the cutter], and
he soon after went onshore to talk with the Chief, King
Terre'boo [Kalani'opu'u], upon the subject. Captain
Cook took with him the Lieutenant, Serjeant and nine
Marines; at his landing he was received with the accustomed respect they upon all occasions paid him, which
more resembled that due to a Deity than a human being
was conducted to the King and they conversed together
with their usual sociality, they were surrounded by a vast
concourse of the Natives who appeared as upon all these
occasions as idle spectators, but there were among them
some very insolent ill-disposed fellows, for one of them
carried his insolence so far, that Captain Cook fired at
him, though in the midst of this mob, with a load of small-
shot, which, though it did no mischief, for the shot were
too small to penetrate the rascals mat he had about him,
still it exceedingly exasperated the whole, producing an
universal Murmur and they soon proceeding to acts of
violence Captain Cook fired a second time and killed a
man when they immediately made a general attack upon
him and his Marines who were drawn up by him; the
Soldiers immediately fired, but before they could reload
their Pieces the Indians [sic] broke in upon them, killed
Captain Cook, four of his party, and wounded the Lieutenant, Serjeant and two others.

There was much about the affair not mentioned by, or
perhaps not known to, Clerke, but for the moment his report

was all that Cook's superiors, family and friends had to go on. Sandwich's reaction on receiving the news was immediate and to the point. There was no discussion of the explorations of the voyage as outlined by Cook in his letter from Unalaska. Instead, Sandwich wrote to Sir Joseph Banks, the botanist on Cook's first voyage who was now President of the Royal Society and a man of power and influence, '... what is uppermost in our minds must always come first, poor Captain Cooke is no more.' Outside the select circle of the Lords of the Admiralty few details of Clerke's letter were revealed. A hurried summary was given to the official *London Gazette* for publication on 11 January, and was copied by other newspapers. It made no mention of the Hawaiians' reverent attitude towards Cook, 'which more resembled that due to a Deity than a human being', but simply referred to Clerke's 'melancholy account' of Cook's death 'on the 14th of February last on the island of O'why'he, one of a group of newly-discovered islands, in an affray with a numerous and tumultuous body of the natives'.

Thus far, deliberately or otherwise, one of the most controversial aspects of Clerke's description of the death of Cook had been kept from the public. This was to change with the issue of the *Morning Chronicle* for 28 January 1780. In St Petersburg James Harris had shown Clerke's letter to the German scientist Peter Simon Pallas, who passed on its contents to the English naturalist Thomas Pennant. From him the details reached the *Morning Chronicle*, and they included the assertion that the Hawaiians had paid Cook 'almost divine honours'. Some indication of official sensitivity came when Sandwich reprimanded Harris for disclosing confidential information, but his reproach was too late. The uncertainty about the circumstances of Cook's death, and indeed what

2. *The Royal Society commemorative medal, designed by Lewis Pingo, chief engraver to the Royal Mint, 1780. The Latin legend reads* Iac. Cook Oceani Investigator Acerrimus *(James Cook most intrepid investigator of the oceans). Of the thirteen gold medals originally struck, one each went to the King, Queen and the Prince of Wales, while another was sent by Sir Joseph Banks to Elizabeth Cook, Captain Cook's widow.*

had happened more generally on the voyage, may explain the lack of any formal move to honour the explorer. It would be wise, one might suppose, to await the return of the ships. Banks, as President of the Royal Society, encouraged the Council of the Society to recognise Cook's achievements as deserving 'some public act', although when on 27 January the Council agreed to issue a commemorative medal in the explorer's honour it made it clear that the cost would fall on individual subscribers, not on the Society. Lewis Pingo, the engraver to the Royal Mint, was chosen to design the medal, which was struck in gold (20 guineas), silver (1 guinea), and bronze (free).

THE GREAT ORONO

Cook's ships arrived at the Cape of Good Hope on their homeward voyage in April 1780, and from there letters and reports were sent to England by fast frigate. By this means the *London Magazine* obtained access to 'authentick Papers' of the voyage and printed an account in July 1780. It contained a few snippets of information about Cook's death that would not have been public knowledge. It had little to say about the expedition's arrival in Hawai'i except, again, that Cook was greeted by the islanders with 'a respect bordering upon adoration', and that the ships were supplied with whatever they needed. Then, on the ships' return, 'suspicion seemed to take the place of hospitality', and after the *Discovery*'s cutter was stolen on 13 February 1779 Cook decided to visit the local chief and demand the boat's return. When the surrounding crowd became threatening, Cook fired his musket at them, but this 'neither did, or was meant to do any mischief'. Cook was then overpowered and killed, along with four of his men.

Following the return of the ships to England the account was revised by an unnamed officer from the voyage in the December 1780 issue of the *London Magazine*, and more detail was added to the death scene. It was now explained that Cook's gun was double-barrelled, one barrel loaded with ball and the other with powder only (in fact, small-shot). The second barrel was the one that he let off at an islander without harming him before he fired the first barrel and killed the leader of his attackers. This provoked an onrush in which Cook was felled by a dagger, and then killed. All this, and more, would soon be available to readers in a variety of articles, pamphlets and books.

In October 1780 the *Resolution* and *Discovery* at last reached the Thames after a voyage which, in the words of Midshipman George Gilbert, had become 'long, tedious and disagreeable'. Within weeks of the ships' return arrangements were being made to publish an authorised account of the voyage. Cook's death twenty months before the end of the voyage made for obvious problems of authorship. Yet public interest, the importance of the expedition's discoveries in the North Pacific, and the Admiralty's uneasiness about the dangers posed by sensational unofficial accounts, ensured that there would be such a book. Up to a point it would be publication by committee, for Banks, Sandwich, the East India Company hydrographer Alexander Dalrymple, and Lieutenant James King from the *Resolution*, were all involved in different ways, advising on place-names, the charts, the engravings. But the main editorial work was entrusted to Dr John Douglas, Canon of St Paul's, who had edited Cook's journal of his second voyage, and who now had the more difficult task of describing the events of a voyage that had lost its dominant personality. To Cook's journal Douglas added the journal kept by the surgeon William Anderson during the first two years of the voyage, while for the events of the voyage after Cook's death he relied mainly on King's journal. Because of production delays, mostly connected with the engravings, the authorised account took almost four years to see the light of day.

Meanwhile, as on the earlier voyages, and despite Admiralty attempts at prohibition, unofficial narratives were written by members of the crew. Intriguingly, William Bligh, Master of the *Resolution*, seems for a time to have been among their number. If he had carried out what King termed 'his threats of printing' it would almost have certainly put an end to any future employment in the Navy, whether in command of the *Bounty* at the time of the famous mutiny or any other vessel. In the event, the first account to appear was an anonymous *Journal of Captain Cook's Last Voyage*, hastily cobbled together and published in May 1781. It was based, in part at least, on a record kept by John Rickman, Second Lieutenant on the *Discovery*. The book was a careless if colourful compilation, but for all its defects it was the first full-length account of the voyage. Extracts from it were published in the widely-read *Gentleman's Magazine* and in the *Critical Review*, while a second London edition and a pirated Dublin edition appeared before the end of the year, and a French edition in 1782. For a year or more it was the only book-length account of Cook's last voyage available to the public. Without any corrective to hand – other than the publisher's cautious note that he was 'not answerable for all the facts' related in the book – readers familiar with the accounts of Cook's first two voyages would have been shocked. Rickman's Cook was a more violent Cook than the generally humane and restrained commander of the earlier voyages. His furious retaliation on Moorea in the Society Islands in October 1777 after the theft of two goats resulted in 'a scene of desolation'. Hundreds of huts and canoes were destroyed, and the plantations cut down, while a terrifying fate seemed to await two youthful hostages on board the ships:

> Every preparation was apparently made for putting them both to death. Large ropes were carried upon the main

deck and made fast fore and aft; axes, chains, and instruments of torture were placed upon the quarter deck in the sight of the young men.

The improbable mock execution scene is not mentioned in any other account, but there is ample evidence that in other ways Cook overreacted on Moorea. The huts and canoes destroyed numbered dozens rather than hundreds, but the loss of the canoes especially was a cruel blow to the islanders' livelihood and pride. Polynesian canoes took many months to build, from the careful selection and felling of trees to the slow construction process by skilled craftsmen, to the solemn day of a ritual launching.

Most interest would have centred on Cook's stay at Kealakekua Bay, after months in which his refusal to land led to 'sullenness and discontent' among the crew. Rickman's book gave readers much food for thought as it described how when the 'King' of Hawai'i came on board the *Resolution* for the first time he fell on his face before Cook 'as a mark of submission'. The next day, when Cook went ashore to pay a return visit, something even more puzzling took place. The King clothed Cook in a robe, placed a garland of plantain leaves on his head, and then led him to an edifice, where, seated on a throne, he became the central figure in a ceremony of worship. As Cook left, the islanders prostrated themselves before him, while for his crew the King's house was known, jocularly or otherwise, as 'Cook's Altar'. This is the first, garbled reference to what in time would become a fully-fledged controversy centring on Cook's supposed worship as a Hawaiian god. Even in Rickman's brief description it is clear that something very odd is happening, that Cook, willingly or otherwise, had stepped outside the normal frame of reference of a Royal Navy captain. One of the Captain's duties, perhaps not always observed conscientiously, was to uphold the tenets 'of the Church of England established by law'. Among the Articles of War that governed life on board a naval vessel, and were regularly read aloud to the assembled crew, the first directed the Captain to hold Sunday divine worship, and the second warned him against permitting the use of blasphemous language by officers and crew or any other behaviour that was 'in derogation of God's honour'.

Baffled readers of this part of Rickman's account would no doubt have hurried on to the climax of the book, the death of Cook. There is no evidence that the writer had witnessed the actual event – on the morning of 14 February Rickman was in charge of boats on the southeast or opposite side of Kealakekua Bay – but from others he related how after the theft of a cutter Cook attempted to take the King hostage, and in the uproar that followed was first felled by a club and then stabbed in the back by a dagger. The book's frontispiece has the first published depiction of the scene of Cook's death, drawn by an unknown artist. Cook is sprawled face-down on the beach, hatless and with his musket fallen from his grasp. The marines are shown fleeing to the water's edge where one of them has turned and is firing point-blank at an attacker. 'Thus ended the life of the greatest navigator that this or any other nation could boast,' Rickman concluded; but the book's reviewer in the *Gentleman's Magazine* was less impressed by the central figure in the drama. Cook's behaviour in taking the King hostage reminded him of a notorious incident from Spain's unsavoury imperial past: 'In the same manner Cortez acted towards Montezuma.'

If we leave out of the reckoning Heinrich Zimmermann's

3. 'The Murder of Capt Cook at O-Why-ee', frontispiece of Journal of Captain Cook's Last Voyage, 1781. This crude engraving shows the marines retreating to the boat while Cook, lying face-down on the beach, is beaten to death with clubs.

brief account in German, published in Mannheim in 1781, the next unofficial narrative of the voyage appeared in 1782 under the name of William Ellis, Surgeon's Mate on the *Discovery*. Based on memory rather than a journal, Ellis's book had little to recommend it. Unlike Rickman's account it received no review in the *Gentleman's Magazine*, while for the *Monthly Review* its publication simply increased the frustration that the authorised account was taking so long to appear. In the section dealing with the expedition's stay in Hawai'i the book made no mention of the islanders' prostration before Cook, or of their apparent worship of him. The description of his death has some detail not found elsewhere, but again it was not first-hand.

Less readily available to readers in Britain than the accounts of Rickman and Ellis was John Ledyard's *A Journal of Captain Cook's Last Voyage,* published in Hartford, Connecticut, in 1783. An American-born marine corporal on the *Resolution,* Ledyard took much of his material from Rickman's book, and what was original has often been discounted because of Ledyard's colonial background. Even so, there is some interesting but unverifiable detail about Cook's first landing at Kealakekua Bay on 17 January 1779:

> The Chief cried out in their language that the great Orono [Lono] was coming, at which they all bowed and covered their faces with their hands until he was passed ... Cook in the mean time improving the awful respect he saw paid him among the natives, permitted himself to be carried upon the shoulders of his bargemen from the boat to the summit of the beach: the bargemen uncovered. As soon as he was set down, the multitude on the beach fell prostrate with their faces to the ground, and their arms extended forward ...

All in all, the unofficial accounts hinted that all was not well on Cook's third voyage. They showed a man given to outbursts of furious temper and vindictive behaviour who was sometimes at odds with his crew, while on Hawai'i he seemed to have allowed, perhaps even encouraged, the islanders' worship of him as a god. Unofficial accounts tended towards the lurid, and a writer in the *Monthly Review* no doubt represented general opinion when he dismissed these 'wanton, petulant, and illiberal attacks' on 'our truly

great navigator', but such criticisms made the delay in publishing an official account of the voyage the more vexing.

APPROACHING TO ADORATION

In June 1784, almost four years after the return of the *Resolution* and *Discovery*, the authorised account of Cook's third
voyage was at last published. By design or coincidence the
day of publication, 4 June, was the King's birthday. The work
was a sumptuous affair, subsidised by the Admiralty, and
dwarfed previous voyage narratives. It ran to three quarto
volumes, 1,617 pages, an atlas, and 87 plates. The compre-
hensiveness of the title seemed a guarantee of its reliability:

A *Voyage to the Pacific Ocean. Undertaken by the Command
of His Majesty, for making Discoveries in the Northern Hemisphere. To determine the Position and Extent of the West Side
of North America: its Distance from Asia and the Practica-
bility of a Northern Passage to Europe. Performed under the
direction of Captains Cook, Clerke and Gore, in His Majesty's
Ships the* Resolution *and* Discovery. *In the Years 1776, 1777,
1778, 1779 and 1780.*

The first two volumes, readers were informed, had been
written by Cook, the third by Captain (Lieutenant during
the voyage) James King. The editor, although not named on
the title page, was Dr John Douglas, FRS, Canon of St Paul's,
who had edited Cook's journal of his second voyage, and
who dedicated the new work 'To the memory of the ablest
and most renowned Navigator this or any other country
hath produced'.

The success of the book was immediate despite its price

of £4 14s. 6d. The *Literary Review* reported that almost the whole printing had been sold on the morning of publication, and the *Monthly Review* added:

> We remember not a circumstance like what has happened on this occasion. On the third day after publication, a copy was not to be met with in the hands of the book-seller; and, to our certain knowledge, six, seven, eight, and even ten guineas, have since been offered for a set.

Frustrated customers unwilling to wait for the reprinting could turn to the cheaper octavo and duodecimo editions. An abridged four-volume octavo edition was quickly published, while a drastically cut one-volume duodecimo edition was also rushed through the press, only to be greeted with derision by reviewers: 'The Iliad in a nut-shell', one complained. One enterprising publisher, George William Anderson, issued accounts of all three of Cook's voyages in eighty affordable sixpenny numbers, which were then brought together in a single handsome folio volume. A rare criticism of the authorised account came from Horace Walpole, that influential commentator on all matters literary, social and political. He had not actually read the book, but one look at the engravings was enough for him: 'a parcel of ugly faces with blubber lips and flat noses ... and rows of savages with backgrounds of palm-trees'.

Others could read the highlights of the voyage in the periodicals. The *Gentleman's Magazine* was especially generous with five monthly instalments; the *Monthly Review* contained four, and the *Critical Review* three. It was a sign of where readers' interests were thought to lie that the first two instalments in the *Gentleman's Magazine* were devoted to

'the transactions immediately preceding, and of the circumstances attending, the final event of Captain Cook's death'.
In the authorised account these 'transactions' began with
the arrival of the *Resolution* and *Discovery* at Kealakekua
Bay on 16 January 1779. That day also saw the last known
entry in Cook's log, a mystifying gap (of which more later).
Having to do without Cook's own record of events, Douglas's account was based on Lieutenant King's journal, kept at
the time, but with revisions made by King himself, together
with additions made from other journals. The resultant
account, detailed and careful, had a long life as the standard
version of Cook's death. Only recently has it become clear
that changes were made to manuscript passages in their
transfer to the published account, some of which amounted
to a manipulation of the record.

There is no reason to suppose that most readers knew or
cared much about such changes. Certainly the reading public
seems to have found the combination of achievement and
tragedy in Cook's final voyage irresistible. Under Douglas's
guiding hand the book told a compelling story of Cook's
stay in Hawai'i. It began with the unprecedented scenes that
greeted the ships' arrival at Kealakekua Bay on 16 January:

> As soon as the inhabitants perceived our intention of
> anchoring in the bay, they came off from the shore in
> astonishing numbers, and expressed their joy by singing
> and shouting, and exhibiting a variety of wild and
> extravagant gestures. The sides, the decks, and rigging
> of both ships were soon completely covered with them;
> and a multitude of women and boys, who had not been
> able to get canoes, came swimming round us in shoals.

4. 'A View of Karakakakooa in Owyhee' by John Webber, 1784. In the
foreground are two double-hulled canoes with lateen sails. Webber's drawing
is dominated by the cliffs of Kealakekua Bay which on the far left descend to
the sea behind the village of Kaawaloa, near where Cook was killed.

King estimated that the ships were surrounded by at least
1,500 canoes and 10,000 islanders, many times more than
the number of people who lived in the area, and all of them
completely unarmed. On none of Cook's earlier Pacific land-
ings had there been a welcome as overwhelming as this.
As the *Resolution* anchored, two chiefs, Palea and Kanina,
came on board accompanied by a priest, Koa'a, who draped
Cook's shoulders with sacred red cloth, offered him a hog,
and recited a long prayer or oration.

In the afternoon Cook and King accompanied Koa'a and
Palea ashore, where the inhabitants of the nearby village of
Hikiau prostrated themselves on the ground as a mark of
adoration. Cook then climbed, although 'not without great
risk of falling', onto a wooden scaffold perched on top of

a great stone *heiau* or shrine, where he was wrapped in red cloth and presented with a hog. As the priests chanted 'Erono' or 'Lono', Cook remained 'aloft, in this awkward situation, swathed round with red cloth, and with difficulty keeping his hold amongst the pieces of rotten scaffolding'. After Cook came down from the ramshackle structure he and King were seated between two idols in a sunken area of the *heiau*, where a procession brought foodstuffs for a ceremonial feast. Cook, who was served by Koa'a,

> could not swallow a morsel; and his reluctance, as may be supposed, was not diminished when the old man, according to his own mode of civility, had chewed it for him.

In the published version we read that Cook left the ceremony 'as soon as he decently could', and returned to the boats, escorted by a procession of attendants bearing wands and chanting 'Erono'. It was, recorded King with some feeling in his manuscript journal, 'a long, & rather tiresome ceremony, of which we could only guess at its Object & Meaning, only that it was highly respectful on their parts'. It was a key moment on the voyage when Cook's record of events, and his understanding of them, would have been invaluable.

There had been a hint of things to come the previous January when the ships first sighted the western islands of the Hawaiian archipelago and Cook landed at Kauai. The moment Cook went ashore, he recorded, several hundred islanders

> all fell flat on their faces, and remained in that humble posture till I made signs to them to rise ... This, as I afterwards understood, is done to their great chiefs.

5. 'An Offering before Capt. Cook in the Sandwich Islands' by John Webber,
1784. The ceremony of 19 January 1779 in which Cook, with his shoulders
covered by red cloth, and accompanied by two of his officers, was presented
with a young hog. Behind the group stand two wooden images, draped
in cloth. On this occasion, unlike the initial ceremony after landing two
days earlier, Cook made certain that Webber was with the party to make a
drawing of the ceremony.

But at Kauai there had been no priests, no elevation at a
heiau, no chanting. There was a different and more puzzling dimension to the landing at Kealakekua Bay, as the

authorised account recognised when it noted that ceremonies on Hawai'i were not only 'expressive of the high respect on the part of the natives', but as far as Captain Cook was concerned 'they seemed approaching to adoration'.

Two days later Cook visited the priests who had been involved in the ceremony at the *heiau*, and whose dwellings were near the observatory that had been set up on the beach. This time he took John Webber, the expedition's artist, to record the event. It was a repetition on a lesser scale of the ceremony on the day Cook landed. Wrapped in red cloth, he was seated below a wooden idol before being presented with a hog, all accompanied by chanting. Whenever Cook went ashore to the observatory he was accompanied in the boat by a priest carrying a wand (the *'tabu* man'), who made sure that those in the nearby canoes stopped paddling and lay face-down until the boat had passed. Once Cook was on shore a chanting priest made the people prostrate themselves and cover their eyes before he was presented with hogs and other foodstuffs, while each day groups took provisions to the shore parties and out to the ships. Again, the authorised account made the point: 'Their presents were made with a regularity, more like a discharge of a religious duty, than the effect of mere liberality.' There were attempts to treat Clerke in a similar way when he went ashore. It is not clear whether his ceremonial reception would have included prostration, for as Clerke characteristically explained he managed to avoid such attentions, 'a very disagreeable kind of amusement'. David Samwell, the Surgeon of the *Discovery* and a keen observer of events, left his readers in no doubt about Cook's special status among the islanders: 'We were universally treated by them with kind attention and hospitality; but the respect they paid to Captain Cook, was little short of adoration.'

On the evening of 25 January, after a *tabu* or prohibition of all activity had been in force over the waters of the bay for two days, the person described in the accounts as the King of the island, Kalani'opu'u, appeared with three great double-hulled canoes from the village of Kaawaloa in the northwest corner of the bay. The chiefs were resplendent in heavy feather cloaks and crested helmets, while priests and their attendants held aloft wickerwork images of their gods. It was a dramatic and colourful occasion drawn by Webber, and one that Cook and his officers had eagerly awaited, but they were taken aback to realise that their visitor was 'the same infirm and emaciated old man' who had come on board the *Resolution*, without much ceremony, while it was off the neighbouring island of Maui the previous November. Lieutenant King was on shore at the observatory, so although Kalani'opu'u remained on board for several hours the authorised account has no details of his encounter with Cook. However, the next day King had a close view of their second meeting when they visited the observatory together. Kalani'opu'u and his chiefs made a magnificent sight in their feathered cloaks and helmets, and were followed by the high priest Kao whose entourage displayed their wickerwork idols on beds of red cloth. Once inside the observatory tent Kalani'opu'u placed his cloak and helmet on Cook, put a feathered wand into his hand, and spread a half-dozen other cloaks at his feet, 'all very beautiful, & to them of the greatest value', King wrote. The two men then exchanged names, 'which amongst all the islanders of the Pacific Ocean, is esteemed the strongest pledge of friendship'. Attendants piled high offerings of food before the two groups went on board the *Resolution*, where Cook presented Kalani'opu'u with a linen shirt and his sword.

6. 'Terreoboo, King of Owhyee, bringing presents to Capt. Cook' by John
Webber, 1784. The scene on 25/26 January 1779 when Kalani'opu'u
approached the Resolution in a great double-hulled canoe, seventy feet long
according to Cook's officers. The King and his chiefs in the leading canoe
are wearing cloaks, while lying in the stern of the canoe on the right are the
recumbent wickerwork figures of Hawaiian gods.

In the authorised account King remembered how relationships with the islanders were more relaxed and infor-
mal away from the grand ceremonies taking place under
the direction of the priests, but in his manuscript journal he
added a warning note: 'Should this respect wear away from
familiarity, or by length of intercourse, their behaviour may
change.' By the beginning of February Kalani'opu'u and
his chiefs were anxiously enquiring when the ships would
leave, and on being told that they would soon sail collected
vast quantities of hogs, sugar cane, yams, sweet potatoes,
plantains and breadfruit. As several journals noted, the
amount of foodstuffs brought to the ships was a huge drain
on the resources of the area, and was ample justification for
the questioning about the ships' departure. On 4 February

the two ships, followed by a fleet of canoes, left Kealakekua Bay. Koa'a, the first priest to greet the ships on their arrival, was still on board the *Resolution*. He acted as pilot as they worked their way along the coast, and before going on shore changed his name to Britannee, 'out of compliment to us'.

HIS HUMANITY PROVED FATAL

Four days out, the *Resolution*'s foremast gave way; and after some hesitation Cook decided to return to Kealakekua Bay, 'all hands much chagrin'd and damning the Foremast'. The ships' reception as they entered the bay on 11 February was very different from their greeting almost a month earlier. In his journal King noted:

> Upon our first Anchoring very few of the Natives came to us. This in some measure hurt our Vanity, as we expected them to flock about us, & to be rejoiced at our return. We were however the less surprised at this, when we were told that it was Taboo for the canoes coming till Terreeo-boo [Kalani'opu'u] returned, who was to pay us a Visit soon.

In the authorised account the pen of either Douglas or King not only gave this passage a more literary turn but also intro-duced an element of foreboding:

> Upon coming to anchor, we were surprized to find our reception very different from what it had been on our first arrival; no shouts, no bustle, no confusion; but a solitary bay, with only here and there a canoe stealing close along the shore ... We were forming various conjectures upon

the occasion of this extraordinary appearance, when our anxiety was at length relieved by the return of a boat which had been sent on shore, and brought us word, that Terreeoboo was absent and had left the bay under the *taboo*. Though this account appeared very satisfactory to most of us; yet others were of opinion, or rather perhaps, have been led, by subsequent events, to imagine, that there was something at this time, very suspicious in the behaviour of the natives.

The next morning Kalani'opu'u came on board the *Resolution*. Without Cook's own account of the encounter, details are few and far between. King was in charge of the shore party setting up the observatory, and the authorised account simply notes that after the visit the islanders resumed 'their former friendly intercourse'. Other records suggest that the meeting may have been a tense one. The journal of Lieutenant James Burney of the *Discovery* noted that the King 'was very inquisitive, as were several of the Owhyhe Chiefs, to know the reason of our return, and appeared much dissatisfied at it'. The keeper of an anonymous journal asserted:

The King ask'd Capt Cook what brought him back again. Cook said his mast was broken. The King told the Capt that he had amused him with lies – that when he [Cook] went away he took his farewell of him and said that he did not know he should ever come again.

By midday on 13 February the ships were once more surrounded by canoes filled with hogs and other foodstuffs, but there was no repetition of the rapturous greetings of the expedition's first visit. Towards evening, scuffles broke out on the beach as stones were thrown at a watering party, and Cook came ashore to the observatory to order King to fire ball (rather than small-shot) if there were any further trouble. Soon after, muskets were fired from the *Discovery* at a canoe heading for shore, and a boat from the ship set off in pursuit. Cook, followed by King and a marine sentry, ran towards the spot where the canoe beached, and when he arrived too late to intercept its occupants set off after them. King's journal relates how in the middle of a huge and noisy crowd Cook made no attempt to wait for King and the marine, or to receive a report from the sailors who had pursued the canoe (and who in fact had recovered the stolen items, the armourer's tongs and chisel). Instead, Cook kept running

> at a great rate along shore ... it was with great difficulty I could at all join him; on coming up to him I askd him if he had heard any tidings of the thief or thing stolen, he said no, but that they point'd a little farther. We kept running on till dark & I believe more than 3 miles from the [observatory] tent, sometimes stopping & enquiring after the thief, the Captn threatening to make the Centry fire, if they did not bring the man. Whenever the Marine made any motion of presenting the Croud would recoil back, but it was observable enough that they began to laugh at our threat.

As darkness closed in, Cook finally gave up the chase but in the gathering gloom was misdirected back to the beach. It was all a far cry from his reception when he first arrived on the island only a month earlier. Little of King's journal entry, with its mixture of the disturbing and the farcical in its description of Cook's undignified chase, found its way into the authorised account. Instead, the whole embarrassing incident was dealt with in a couple of sentences.

On Cook's return to the observatory he learned that the crew of the boat waiting to take him back to the ship had become involved in a quarrel over the beached canoe, which belonged to Palea, who was by now known to be the King's *'aikane* or male lover. In the fracas the chief was laid out by a blow from an oar before volleys of stones from a crowd gathered on the beach forced the pinnace's unarmed crew to abandon their boat. Only Palea's intervention after he recovered consciousness saved two of the crew from a beating and the pinnace from destruction. Even so, all but one of the pinnace's oars were smashed. Cook returned on board the *Resolution* 'exceeding angry', and cleared the ship of all islanders, both men and women, telling King before he left that 'the behaviour of the Indians would at last oblige him to use force'.

At daylight King returned to the *Resolution*, but as he passed the *Discovery* he learned that her large cutter had been stolen some time before dawn. This was the most daring and serious theft on any of Cook's voyages, for the cutter was the ship's biggest and most useful boat. When King reached the *Resolution* he found the marines arming, while Cook, loading a double-barrelled musket with ball and small-shot, was not interested in details of the previous day's scuffle. 'We are not arming for that last nights affair,' he told King. 'They have stolen the Cutter, & it is for that we are making preparations.' At about 7 a.m. the two men left the ship, Cook in the pinnace with Lieutenant Molesworth Phillips and nine marines to the village of Kaawaloa where Kalani'opu'u was in residence, King back to the observatory where he was to continue his astronomical work.

The authorised account maintained that Cook intended to follow 'his usual practice' of taking the principal chief of the area hostage until the stolen goods were returned. At the same time the ships' boats were to stop any canoes leaving the bay. Clerke's journal, however, has no mention of hostage-taking. It simply records that Cook's reaction when he heard of the theft of the cutter was to send the *Resolution*'s boats to the northwest side of the bay, and the *Discovery*'s to the southeast, to confine or seize all canoes in sight, and that he 'made no doubt but to redeem them they would very readily return the Boat'. Clerke then went back to the *Discovery* to give orders to this effect, sending Rickman and a party of marines with the launch and small cutter to the southeast side of the bay. He then returned to the *Resolution* to have 'some more discourse with Capt Cook upon this business', only to be told that Cook, rather than sending his boats on blockade duty, had recalled his launch and had taken it, together with the pinnace, to Kaawaloa. The news surprised Clerke, but as he was rowed back to the *Discovery* he reassured himself with the thought that 'as Capt Cook was gone to the King, matters would soon be settled, for we were as yet by no means upon bad terms either with Arees [chiefs] or any body else'.

Soon after getting on board the *Discovery* Clerke first heard musket-fire from Rickman's boats, and then shouting and firing from the shore where Cook had landed. 'With my Glass I clearly saw that our People were drove off to their Boats but I could not distinguish Persons in that confused Croud'. Then news reached the *Discovery* that 'Capt Cook and four Marines had fallen in this confounded Affray', and an exhausted Clerke (so weak that at times he could not take the deck of his ship), was once again rowed to the *Resolution*, this time to assume command. On board he found Molesworth Phillips, wounded in the back but able to describe what had happened on shore.

When Cook landed near the village of Kaawaloa that morning he met Kalani'opu'u's two young sons, who took him to the hut where their father was sleeping. When he awoke, he agreed to accompany Cook to the beach, where his sons were already in the pinnace and where the marines were now drawn up in line near the water's edge. Cook's plan to return to the ship with the King was thwarted when Kalani'opu'u was persuaded by one of his wives, the mother of the boys, and two chiefs, to sit on the ground, and remained there despite all Cook's efforts. With a large crowd gathering at the scene, Cook decided to abandon the attempt. It was at this time that news seems to have reached the crowd that a chief had been shot dead in his canoe by the *Discovery*'s blockading boats (commanded by Rickman). At this, the crowd was 'thrown into a great rage & ferment', the women and children were sent away, and the men put on defensive mats and armed themselves with spears and stones. When one threatened Cook with a stone and a dagger Cook fired, but the small-shot failed to penetrate the man's wicker mat. As stones were thrown and one of the chiefs tried to stab Phillips, Cook fired the other barrel of his musket, loaded with ball, and killed a man. This drew further volleys of stones, answered by musket-fire from the marines and from the boats lying just offshore, commanded by Lieutenant Williamson. There is a significant difference here between Phillips's account as related by Clerke and the version in the authorised account. In the former, as the stones were thrown 'the Capt gave orders to the Marines to fire'; in the latter Cook momentarily disappears from the scene and we read only that the stone-throwing 'was answered by a discharge of musquetry from the marines, and the people in the boats'. This difference of emphasis is reflected in King's journal as he tries to reconcile the various accounts:

> It is said by some that he [Cook] now orderd the Marines to fire which was follow'd by the boats; others that the boats fir'd first. Be it as it may, the Captn calld to them to cease fyring & to come in with the Boats, intending to embark as fast as Possible.

What followed, according to the authorised account, 'was a scene of the utmost horror and confusion'. Cook was stabbed in the back by a dagger and fell face-down in the water (Samwell maintained that he was first struck down by a large club), while several marines, including Phillips, were wounded. The Lieutenant managed to scramble through the shallows to the pinnace, but made it clear that 'after being knock'd down I saw no more of Capt Cook'. Nowhere was there any mention of one of the ironies of the death scene, that the fearsome weapon that stabbed Cook was one of those manufactured on the ships, and used as gifts or trade goods on the island. As Burney explained in his journal, they were 'Iron Spikes from 18 Inches to 2½ feet long, worked in the form of their own wooden Daggers ... called *Pahooah*'. Clerke recalled that he had presented one of the iron daggers to Kalani'opu'u the evening before Cook's death, while if Johann Reinhold Forster is to be trusted (he was not on the voyage) the dagger that struck down Cook had been given by him to his assailant earlier in the stay.

In reflecting on the whole miserable affair Clerke had no doubt that the crucial mistake was Cook's decision to open fire, confident that this would disperse the crowd. As he left the *Resolution* that morning, Cook reassured the crew of the cutter that there would be no serious resistance from the islanders, 'for he was very positive the Indians would not stand the fire of a single musket'. Cook's firm belief in the effectiveness of this 'last resource', on this occasion at least, was ill-founded, not least because he first fired small-shot rather than the more lethal ball. A year earlier, Williamson had shot dead a chief at Kauai, and the justification in his journal for using ball on that occasion has an oddly prophetic ring to it when the events at Kealakekua Bay are considered:

C[aptain]n Cook & I entertain'd very different opinions upon ye manner of treating indians. He asserts that he always found upon his first going among them, that ye firing wth small-shot answers ye purpose, but C[aptai]n Clerke & many of ye Officers that have sail'd with him, declare, that ye firing with small-shot always had bad effects.

Clerke had been told that a few minutes before the violence began the crowd had readily cleared a way for the marines to reach the beach, where they drew up in order, and he argued that if an attack had been planned then it would have been made when the marines were 'in the midst of the Mob'. Clerke's informant was probably Phillips, and an intriguing fragment of later evidence tends to support this. In 1849 Phillips's own journal of the voyage was in the possession of one Christopher Kreest. It had apparently been returned to Phillips by the Admiralty after the publication of the authorised account in 1784. As he sent it to a friend to read Kreest commented, 'Pray, take care of the Book, You will

find Phillips's account of the death of Capt Cooke interesting
… as it shows that *he* (not the Islanders), was the assailant.'
Unfortunately, despite Kreest's exhortation, the journal has
vanished.

Nothing of Clerke's view appeared in the authorised
account, which instead relied on King. Like Clerke, King was
too far away from Kaawaloa to have any clear sense of events
there, but he also made his own enquiries once he was back
on the *Resolution*. Cook, he felt, had become over-confident
in his handling of native peoples, and had lost 'that wise distrust he formerly had'. This complacency was strengthened
by the welcome given to the ships on their first arrival at
Kealakekua Bay, and accounted for the failure to react to the
changed mood when the ships returned. The fact that this
change was 'hardly observed or attended to' was couched
in general terms by King, but it was an implicit criticism of
Cook. All in all, as Kerry Howe has written, 'Among the sad-
dened crews in Kealakekua Bay, there was considerable sentiment that Cook had contributed to his own death.'

King found that collecting evidence about the fracas was
not a straightforward business, for 'the accounts that were
given now begin to differ'. One element in this was the pro-
tective urge of individuals when they set down their recollections in writing to absolve themselves from any blame for
the catastrophe on the beach. Reputations, friendships, even
future promotions, were all at stake. In terms of substance
the accounts differed on the fundamental issue of whether
Cook's death came about through his aggressive behaviour
in attempting to take Kalani'opu'u hostage and firing into the
crowd; or whether it was the unfortunate consequence of what
one crew member called his 'ill timed restraint' in using, first,
only small-shot, and then ordering the boat crews to cease

firing. King noted that when Cook was struggling to reach the water's edge he tried to repel his assailants with the butt end of his musket, but the significant passage in his journal as it appeared in the authorised account ran as follows:

> Our unfortunate Commander, the last time he was seen distinctly, was standing at the water's edge, and calling out to the boats to cease firing, and to pull in. If it be true, as some of those present have imagined, that the marines and boatmen had fired without his orders, and that he was desirous of preventing any further bloodshed, it is not improbable that his humanity, on this occasion, proved fatal to him. For it was remarked, that whilst he faced the natives, none of them had offered him any violence, but that having turned about, to give his orders to the boats, he was stabbed in the back, and fell with his face into the water.

This became the official version of the death of Cook, but as Nicholas Thomas has written, the different interpretations of the day 'prefigured argument that has, like an incurable wound, broken open from time to time ever since', with the two sides divided on the issue of whether Cook died because of his excessive anger or his excessive humanity.

WHAT OUR FEELINGS WERE, I LEAVE THE WORLD TO CONCEIVE

On board the ships there was little agreement as to how to respond to the killing of Cook and the four marines. When the boats reached the *Resolution* with the news of Cook's death, Midshipman Gilbert recalled that a general silence ensued throughout the ship for the space of near half an hour: it appearing to some of us somewhat like a Dream that we could not reconcile ourselves to.

As the shock wore off calls for revenge by some were met by others with arguments based on caution and humanity. All agreed that a priority was the recovery of Cook's body, but this was not an easy task. Under cover of darkness on the night of the 15th a canoe holding two men approached the *Resolution*, one of them the *tabu* man who had accompanied Cook everywhere with his wand. Two nervous sentries fired their muskets at the canoe, although without hitting either man. King's journal entry of what happened next was repeated with little change in the authorised account:

After lamenting, with abundance of tears, the loss of *Orono*, he told us that he had brought us a part of his body. He then presented to us a small bundle wrapped up in cloth, which he brought under his arm; and it is impossible to describe the horror which seized us on finding in it a piece of human flesh, about nine or ten pounds weight. This, he said, was all that remained of the body; that the rest was cut to pieces and burnt.

A few days later King learned that most of Cook's burnt remains had been ceremonially distributed among the great chiefs, the mark of honour paid to a dead adversary of high status.

Among other news that the men brought was that seventeen islanders had been killed at Kaawaloa the previous day, and another eight elsewhere. Then, 'A Singular question was askd by them, & that was when the Erono would return, this was demanded afterwards by others, & what he would do to them when he return'd.' To the puzzled crew members it was becoming clear that their dead captain was the islanders' 'Orono' or 'Lono', and as such immortal and possibly vengeful. The conversation was repeated in the authorised account, but the only attempt at explanation carefully avoided any reference to Cook's possible godlike status with the comment that 'they considered him as a being of a superior nature'.

King, both in his journal and in the authorised account, made no attempt to gloss over the retributive behaviour of the crews, although he also stressed the provocative behaviour of the islanders. On 16 February one man paddled near the ship, hurling stones and waving Cook's tattered hat over his head, to the cheers of the crowds on shore. 'Our people,' King wrote, 'were all in a flame at this insult,' and Clerke ordered the ship's four-pounders to open fire. But the main retaliation came the next day, when orders to burn a few huts from which men were throwing stones at a watering party turned into something altogether more destructive. Clerke's journal was fairly laconic:

> In the Afternoon the Boats return'd to the Watering business and as the Natives continued troublesome we burnt down the Town that was at the head of the Beach which depriv'd them of their principal shelter.

King, who would normally have been in charge of this operation but who was ill, described what happened. The whole village near the *heiau* was set on fire, and many of those escaping the flames were shot. Other journals reported that two of the dead were decapitated, and their heads stuck on poles and brought back to the ship. All this found its way into the authorised account, where King, although not going as far as his journal, where he admitted that sailors could 'equal the Cruelty of the most savage indian', referred to 'acts of unnecessary cruelty and devastation'.

On the 20th a ceremonial procession preceded by two drummers came down to the beach, followed by a chief, Hiapo, 'bearing something with great solemnity in his hands'. When opened, the bundle was found to contain Cook's hands, most of the skull, the bones of his arms, and his leg bones. The next day further bones were brought on board, together with the barrels of his musket, his shoes, and some other oddments. A week after their captain's death it was now time for the crew to bury what was left of him. King's journal is curiously casual about the occasion:

> We told Yappo [Hiapo] to Tabboo all the bay, as we should fire Guns on burying the Captn, which might do mischief; accordingly in the Afternoon we had the Service read over the bones which were put into a Coffin & thrown into the Sea.

That there was more to it than this is shown by the log kept by Thomas Edgar, Master of the *Discovery*:

> At 5 both Ships hoisted Ensign's and Pendant half Staff up & Crossd over Yards, at ½ past the Resolution toll'd her bell & fir'd 10 four pounders half Minute Gun's & committed the bones of Capt: Cooke to the Deep.

For the published account King realised that something a little more dignified was needed than his offhand journal entry:

> Nothing now remained, but to perform the last offices to our great and unfortunate commander. Eappo was dismissed with orders to *taboo* all the bay; and in the afternoon, the bones having been put into a coffin, and the service read over them, they were committed to the deep with the usual military honours. What our feelings were on this occasion, I leave the world to conceive.

The next day the ships left Kealakekua Bay. It was, wrote King, a place marked by 'the very unfortunate, & Tragical death of one of the greatest Navigators our Nation or any Nation ever had'.

THE PUBLIC NEVER KNEW, HOW MUCH THEY OWE TO ME

The publication of the official account of Cook's third voyage edited by Dr Douglas set the seal on the explorer's fame. Until J.C. Beaglehole's scholarly edition of the manuscript journals of the voyage in the mid-twentieth century it remained the standard account, the deep quarry from which generations of readers and writers took their materials as they struggled to understand what had happened on Cook's last voyage. The question therefore of how much of the published work was Cook's and how much his editor's is crucial. Those critics such as the writer of a letter to the *Morning Chronicle* on 18 January 1783 who complained that the narratives of published voyages such as Anson's and Cook's would have been better told in the navigators' own words were reassured by Douglas that Cook's journal, now in the British Library, 'which exists in his own hand-writing, has been faithfully adhered to'. That this was not quite the case is shown by a note written after publication by Douglas who, clearly stung by the lack of recognition for his editorial efforts, complained, 'The Public never knew, how much they owe to me in this work.' He went on to say, 'The Capt's M.S.S. was my Ground work,' before realising that this was perhaps claiming too much. The sentence was crossed out and replaced by a longer passage:

> The Capt's M.S.S. was indeed attended to accurately, but I took more Liberties than I had done with his Acct of the second Voyage; and while I faithfully represented the facts, I was less scrupulous in cloathing them with better Stile than fell to the usual Share of the Capt.

The editorial process can be clearly seen in Douglas's own copy of Cook's journal, which is interspersed on almost every page with editorial additions and revisions to the explorer's text. This copy, in two volumes, also in the British Library, seems not to have been noticed by Cook scholars, yet it provides clear evidence of how Douglas set about his task. A comparison of Cook's manuscript journal and the published version as edited by Douglas reveals a host of revisions, some minor and stylistic, others more drastic. One of Douglas's most significant editorial amplifications altered the emphasis of a passage written by Cook during his stay at Nootka Sound on the west coast of Vancouver Island. In a brief mention Cook included 'human sculs and hands' among the items offered by the Nootka as trade goods. In the published version this was enlarged to something altogether more meaningful:

But the most extraordinary of all the articles which they brought to the ships for sale, were human skulls, and hands not yet quite stripped of the flesh, which they made our people plainly understand they had eaten; and, indeed, some of them had evident marks that they had been upon the fire.

Elsewhere, changes were made that afforded Cook powers of hindsight that he never claimed in his manuscript journal. When in August 1778 Cook first sailed through Bering Strait he was uncertain whether the shore to the west was part of Asia or Alaska. His subsequent track in the Arctic Ocean pointed to the former, and on his return through the strait Cook wrote, 'I was now assured that this was ... the NE coast of Asia.' In the published version this read, 'I was now well assured, *of what I had believed before* [my italics], that this was ... the North East coast of Asia.'

Throughout the published edition the syntax of Cook's journal was altered to stress the role of the first-person narrator, the commanding officer who is forever ordering, directing, mastering. Douglas's Cook is heroic and just, stern but compassionate. As he surveys, charts, takes possession, he is the representative of the monarch, the flag-bearer of a patriotic imperialism that few questioned. One of Douglas's changes had the effect of removing any imputation of insubordination or disloyalty by Cook. The original journal entry for 19 December 1778 contained a long complaint by Cook about the quality of the cordage and canvas supplied by the naval dockyards to his vessels. An anxious Douglas consulted Sir Hugh Palliser, Comptroller of the Navy and one of the most influential of Cook's patrons, who advised that part of the entry should be deleted since it seemed 'to convey a complaint of abuse or mismanagement in the Yards which is improper in Capt Cook in such a Work'. In his own copy of Cook's journal, Douglas pasted in a sheet incorporating Palliser's suggested wording, and so it appears in the published account. On the other hand, Douglas left in, with some alterations, a critical entry earlier in the month by Cook about the refusal of his 'Mutinous crew' to drink sugar-cane beer, although most of the entry had been crossed out by Cook or some other person in the holograph journal.

For the weeks in Hawai'i, when he no longer had Cook's journal to draw upon, Douglas was highly selective in his use of materials from other journals. We have seen how King's journal has a detailed account of the incident the evening before Cook's death when he, Cook and a marine, chased and lost a suspected thief, accompanied by the derisive laughter of onlookers. In the authorised account this humiliating episode is quickly dismissed. The next day, when Captain Clerke went on board the *Resolution* after the theft of the *Discovery's* cutter, Cook seems not to have mentioned to him his intention to take Kalani'opu'u hostage, a fact again glossed over by Douglas. In his description of the death of Cook and the marines Douglas made much of Cook's humanity in ordering the boats to stop firing, but omitted Phillips's recollection that it was Cook who had given the order to fire in the first place. And totally missing from the authorised account was mention of the discreditable behaviour of John Williamson, Third Lieutenant of the *Resolution*, who was in command of the launch lying just offshore, but who inexplicably chose to interpret Cook's arm-waving as an order to pull away from the beach rather than come to his assistance. Edward Thompson, a naval captain who heard details of the affair from King after the expedition's return to England, was furious at the silence of the authorised account: 'He [Cook] lost his life, by not being supported by Lieut. Williamson, who shoved off the boats, yet no word is mentioned of it.'

One should not assume that Cook's manuscript journal is a full and frank record of events, and that Douglas and Palliser were the only revisers. There was a fair amount of censorship by Cook himself. He was writing, in the first instance, for the Lords of the Admiralty, but also for posterity in the shape of the published account that was to come. Even allowing for the fact that much took place on shore and even on shipboard beyond the sight and hearing of the captain, there were significant glosses and omissions in Cook's journal that cannot be attributed to Douglas. We read little in it about the increasingly severe punishments meted out to thieves in Tonga, while full details of the destruction of canoes in Moorea were left for others to record. There was nothing novel in using the published account of a voyage as an apologia. The voyages earlier in the century by William Dampier, Woodes Rogers and George Anson all produced books intended to justify the actions of the expedition's commanding officer. A common characteristic of such accounts was their claim to straightforward, honest language, so Cook's introduction to his journal of his second voyage, which would be published in 1777 as *A Voyage towards the South Pole, and Round the World*, followed well-established precedents, as he explained:

It is a work for information and not for amusement, written by a man, who has not the advantage of Education, acquired, nor Natural abilities for writing; but by one who has been constantly at sea from his youth, and who, with the Assistance of a few good friends gone through all the Stations belonging to a Seaman, from a prentice boy in the Coal Trade to a Commander in the Navy. After such a Candid confession he hopes the Public will not consider him as an author, but a man Zealously employed in the Service of his Country, and obliged to give the best account he is able of his proceedings.

As Philip Edwards has written, the aim of such protestations was to give the impression of 'manly tars gripping their pens in fists more accustomed to handling ropes, setting down their recollections in simple and conscientious honesty'. Dampier and Rogers were concealing much that happened on their fraught and chaotic expeditions, and even in the case of Cook's well-managed second voyage there was something rather ingenuous about his authorial depreciation. On that voyage, Cook kept almost a superfluity of logs and journals – a log and two journals in his own handwriting, and no fewer than three clerical copies, as well as some individual sections and fragments. The process of composition began with the daily log/journal entries, written as close to the event as possible; but that record was only the beginning, and on both his second and third voyages Cook did a great deal of rewriting in order to produce a journal that would satisfy himself, the Lords of the Admiralty, and the readers of the published edition.

HERE CAPTAIN COOK'S JOURNAL ENDS

The number of different logs and journals routinely kept by Cook makes all the more mystifying the total lack on the third voyage of any known record by him covering his stay on Hawai'i in January and February 1779 – arguably the most

critical weeks of his naval career. Until that time Cook's jour-
nal-keeping resembled that on his second voyage, and at first
sight the records seem plentiful. The prime source, the journal
in his own hand, is a bulky quarto volume of more than 600
folios with the journal entries written on the facing (or *recto*)
page of the folio while the back (or *verso*) page was generally
left blank. It begins with Cook going on board the *Resolution*
at Deptford to take up his command on 10 February 1776,
and ends on 6 January 1779 off the southern tip of Hawai'i,
more than a week before the fateful landing at Kealakekua
Bay. Although not a 'clean' copy, for there are deletions, inser-
tions and blank spaces, this volume was clearly intended to
serve as the basis for the published account of the voyage.
Technical matters were kept to a minimum, the entries are
in civil time*, and days when little happens are telescoped
together. Its last entry describes Captain Clerke coming on
board the *Resolution* when the *Discovery* rejoined Cook on
6 January after a thirteen-day separation off Hawai'i. The
journal ends suddenly, without explanation, that day, two-
thirds of the way down the volume's penultimate folio. The
last folio is blank. There is a similar cut-off point in the clerical copy of the journal among the Admiralty records in the
National Archives, and in the revised two-volume version of
the journal in Douglas's hand.

The British Library, however, also holds a further record
covering the next eleven days, part of a log in Cook's hand in
four large folio sheets, running from 28 November 1778 to 17

*Until 1805 nautical time differed from civil time in that the
twenty-four-hour day extended from noon to noon, not midnight to
midnight. Thus, entries for 12 May in a seaman's log would cover
the afternoon and night of 11 May (civil time) and the morning of 12
May (civil time).

7. *The last page of Captain Cook's log, 17 January 1779, showing the unfinished or interrupted nature of the record.*

January 1779. Its entries are briefer than those in the journal, but with more nautical detail, and kept in ship's time. It is possible that this section was part of the daily log that would have been kept by Cook throughout the voyage. There is a reference to 'two Volumes of the Log' after the ships returned to London. We know that Douglas had this in his possession while he was preparing Cook's journal for publication, for in a marginal note in his own edited copy of the journal he refers to Cook's 'Log Book', and takes information from it which is not in the journal. This substantial record has disappeared. The final entry of the log fragment ends three-quarters of the way down the page, at the moment of Cook going ashore at Kealakekua Bay for the first time on the afternoon of 17 January (16 January civil time). The last words we have in Cook's hand read:

> I went a shore to view the place, accompanied by Touahah [the priest Koa'a], Parea [the chief Palea], Mr King and others; as soon as we landed Touahah took me by the hand and conducted me to a large Morai, the other gentlemen with Parea and four or five more of the Natives followed.

It ends, that is, in mid-episode, just as Cook was about to be led to the *marae* (Cook used the Tahitian term) or *heiau*, surrounded by thousands of islanders prostrating themselves.

After Clerke's death in August 1779 command of the expedition devolved upon Gore, and with it care of the ship's papers. When he arrived at the Cape of Good Hope, Gore sent Cook's journal home by a fast frigate at the beginning of May 1780. However, by this time the Admiralty had already received a copy of the journal that had been entrusted by

Clerke to Magnus von Behm, the Governor of Kamchatka, while the *Resolution* and *Discovery* were at Petropavlovsk in May 1779. This reached St Petersburg by overland route in March 1780, and was forwarded to London by the Ambassador, Sir James Harris. We know that two copies were made of Cook's journal, so the probability is that one was sent to London from the Cape, and the other from Kamchatka, while the original in Cook's own hand was kept by Gore until the *Resolution* reached home waters. There is some evidence – not very strong – that there was some meddling with Cook's journal while it was in Gore's custody. In February 1784 James King replied to a query from Douglas about the deletion of the entry concerning the crew's refusal to drink sugar-cane beer:

> I saw Capt. Cooks M.S. the day after his death & the part giving an account of the mutinous refusal to drink the sugar cane beer was not then erased; and I am almost confident that that part was not erased in Capt. Clerke's time, but after C. Gore got possession of the M.S.

The most frustrating gap in the paper trail is revealed in letters between Douglas, King and Philip Stephens, Secretary to the Admiralty. On 14 November 1780 Stephens told Douglas that he was sending him three parcels of 'Capt. Cooks Journals Log Books & loose Manuscripts relative to this Voyage'. A month later King wrote to Douglas:

> I have made all the enquiries but without effect for Capt. Cook's loose papers, they are not at the Admiralty, Mrs Cook has not got them & the Clerke knows nothing of them.

What exactly had disappeared is not easy to tell from this exchange. One possibility is that two of the parcels containing logs and journals reached Douglas, and that it was only the third parcel containing 'loose papers' that had gone astray. Alternatively, it could be that all three parcels had disappeared, thus accounting for the several logs and journals we know are missing as well as the elusive 'loose papers'. All in all, as Beaglehole has observed, 'We can only feel that too many manuscripts in Cook's hand, or copies of them, too many "loose papers", were allowed to disappear.'

This mild complaint has encouraged suspicions that there had been a weeding of the record, and especially that dealing with Cook's weeks at Kealakekua Bay. Anne Salmond has speculated that when Clerke took command of the expedition he destroyed the last section of Cook's journal because it 'included compromising material'. In this context a passage in David Samwell's published account of Cook's death might have some relevance. Writing about Williamson's conduct on the day of Cook's death, Samwell recorded that complaints about the Lieutenant were so loud

> as to oblige Captain Clerke publickly to notice them, and to take the depositions of his accusers down in writing. The Captain's bad state of health and approaching dissolution, it is supposed, induced him to destroy these papers a short time before his death.

Even if Samwell's guess was correct, it would be one thing for Clerke to destroy his own notes, quite another to do away with the official record kept by Cook, and one that it would be difficult to conceal from the other officers on the *Resolution*. Gananath Obeyesekere has recently pointed

the finger of blame higher up the ladder of authority. He
writes:

> My own suspicious mind assumes that these logs (and
> also other Cook papers) contained so much damaging
> evidence of Cook's violence that they were deliberately
> 'lost' by the Admiralty. Shredding of damaging evidence
> is an old custom.

It must be said that since the only part of Cook's journal
missing in its entirety is that dealing with his stay in Hawai'i,
then it was less his 'violence' (not much in evidence before
14 February) than his apparent worship as a god that might
embarrass the Admiralty, especially if Cook's own entries
revealed that he had encouraged the adulation he received.
It was, after all, Cook who set the tone for the published
account of his second voyage when he reminded Douglas
that it must be 'unexceptionable to the nicest readers', and
that 'nothing indecent may appear in the whole book'. It
would be hard to imagine anything more indecent to readers
in a Britain coming increasingly under the influence of evangelical groups than the thought of the country's foremost
explorer accepting a status as a heathen god. The Quaker
community in which Cook spent some of his formative
years in Whitby disapproved of priests, ceremonials, even
pulpits, and although Quakers were admittedly a small
minority, God-fearing Protestants everywhere abhorred the
worship of 'graven images', and would recoil in horror from
any identification of Cook with the pagan idols of Hawai'i.
It is a sign of the sacrilegious implications of that possibility
that none of the journal-keepers could quite bring himself
to state outright that Cook was treated as a god. All edged

around the issue, with broad hints rather than direct asser-
tions. So Clerke – 'respect which more resembled that due to
a Deity than a human being'; Ledyard – 'the awful respect
paid him'; King – 'approaching to adoration'; Samwell –
'partaking something of divinity'. From the time of Spain's
early contacts with the Americas there had been examples of
the leaders of the invaders being regarded as ancestral gods
by many within indigenous societies; the crucial question as
far as Cook was concerned was whether in 1779 he had actually encouraged the Hawaiians' worship. Given the absence
of Cook's own record of events, how far he accepted or even
recognised what was happening is uncertain, although the
matter exercised many commentators in later years. It is just
conceivable that at the welcoming ceremony on the afternoon of his arrival at Kealakekua Bay he believed from his
experiences elsewhere in Polynesia that the sacrifices and
gifts were customary offerings to the wooden idols at the
heiau rather than to him, although his swathing in red cloth,
his lofty position on the wooden edifice, the mass prostrations and the chanting, make it difficult to accept that this
assumption was anything but momentary. The most sympathetic interpretation of Cook's acquiescence is that he wel-
comed the practical advantages of his unexpected elevation,
advantages that were confirmed by each canoe-load of provisions brought out to the ships.

Two pieces of evidence at first sight seem to support
the possibility that Douglas had in his possession more
of Cook's journal than was published. A journalist in the
Monthly Review for June 1782 wrote of the planned official
account: 'The narrative will be printed from that celebrated
navigator's own account; which, it seems, was complete to
the evening before his death.' This is intriguing, but it could

well have been a speculative guess rather than an assertion based on hard evidence. A second oddity is that, according to Douglas's editorialised version of Cook's journal, Cook's last written words described not his going ashore at Kealakekua Bay on the afternoon of 17 January 1779, but the tumultuous arrival of the ships in the bay a few hours earlier:

> We could not but be struck with the Singularity of this scene; and perhaps there were few on board who now lamented our having failed in our Endeavours to find a Northern Passage homeward, last Summer. To this disappointment we owed our having it in our Power to revisit the Sandwich Islands, and to enrich our Voyage with a Discovery which, though the last, seemed, in many Respects, to be the most important that had hitherto been made by Europeans, throughout the Extent of the Pacific Ocean.

This is followed by Douglas's comment, 'Here Captain Cook's journal ends,' although the passage just quoted is not found either in Cook's manuscript journal or in the log fragment.

It raises the possibility, one might think, that Douglas had in front of him at least one further copy of Cook's journal, and accidentally allowed two sentences from it to stray into print – evidence of a decision to conceal Cook's journal entries describing his stay on Hawai'i. However, closer examination of the wording of the extra piece of text in the published account throws doubt on whether it was actually written by Cook. It is difficult to see how Cook in January 1779 could assert that the Sandwich Islands were the 'last' of his discoveries since at that time he was preparing to return to northern waters in another attempt to find the Northwest Passage. Unlikely though that discovery might now be, it would put all other achievements of the voyage in the shade. Rather more probable is that the resounding sentences were added by Douglas to make a suitable conclusion to the dead explorer's journal. This supposition that the extra sentences were Douglas's rather than Cook's is strengthened by the fact that they were, unusually, repeated without any modification in the published account.

It is difficult to accept the scenario of a final journal that was deliberately destroyed, for there were too many involved in the collecting and collating of Cook's papers in London for such a disappearance to be easily managed or kept secret. But if this possibility is dismissed, then the central puzzle remains why Cook ended both his journal and his log so abruptly – in mid-air, so to speak. The hiatus in the journal can perhaps be explained. At more than 600 pages in Cook's own hand the volume represented a monumental effort of composition and writing. To enable additional information to be inserted, or second thoughts to be expressed, it would make sense to record events, for the time being, in a less formal fashion, and to transfer the entries to his journal after due consideration. If for the weeks of the vessels' slow approach to Kealakekua Bay that less formal record was the log (of which we have only a fragment), then its abrupt closure is less easy to explain. Unlike the more polished journal the log was written on the spot, with the names of islands and other natural features left blank, and with none of the hindsight often displayed in the journal. And if it is accepted that Cook sometimes wrote his journal well after the event, the six-week gap from 6 January to the day of his death on 14 February 1779 would seem to be an extraordinarily long one, especially given the fact that the ships were in harbour for much of the time, when Cook would have more leisure than normal to bring his journal up to date.

As we have seen, the fragment of log ends during the afternoon of 16/17 January as Cook landed and was led along the shore to the *heiau*. To repeat its final entry:

> I went a shore to view the place, accompanied by Touahah, Parea, Mr King and others; as soon as we landed Touahah took me by the hand and conducted me to a large Morai, the other gentlemen with Parea and four or five more of the Natives followed.

Presumably, Cook wrote these words when he returned to the *Resolution* that evening; the question is why he stopped his record after his description of the approach to the *heiau*. King's journal perhaps provides an answer. Spreading himself over several pages, King described first how when Cook landed he was greeted with the word 'Erono' while the islanders prostrated themselves before him. This was the scene that Cook would have had to describe next in his log before moving on to his climb up the wooden scaffold and the subsequent 'long, & rather tiresome ceremony, of which we could only guess at its Object & Meaning' (King's words). On board ship after all this, no doubt tired, almost certainly puzzled, and perhaps uneasy, Cook stopped writing in his log after only a few lines. When Cook picked up his pen again is not known, and his decision when he did that he would abandon the journal and log he had been keeping thus far is hard to explain. It would seem inconceivable for Cook as commander of the expedition not to continue his record of events – to keep a daily log was one of the prime requirements of any naval captain – but all that can be said is that it is in none of the documents that survive. Whether his log entries after 16 January 1779 were kept in the 'loose papers' that were later lost we have no way of telling. If they were contained in the logbook that disappeared after being in Douglas's possession it is difficult to understand why the editor did not include them in the authorised account. Neither Douglas nor the Admiralty comes well out of this business. Douglas held on to journals and logs that were official property, and for its part the Admiralty seems to have made no attempt to retrieve them. They were not relinquished by the Douglas family until 1872, when they were sold to the British Museum. If there was a conspiracy, it was a conspiracy of silence in which neither Cook's officers nor his editor seem to have been interested enough to remark on the curious business of the missing entries. It is especially odd that James King, joint author of the authorised account, who 'saw Capt. Cooks M.S. the day after his death', had nothing to say on the subject.

The disappearance of Cook's own record allowed Douglas and his advisers at the Admiralty to portray the story of the stay at Hawai'i as they wished. King's journal formed the basis for the final volume of the authorised account, but Douglas in consultation with Banks and the Lords of the Admiralty decided how it should appear. In the end, Douglas's edition offered more than an apologia for a voyage with some awkward moments – it played a major part in establishing Cook as a hero.

2

AN ENLIGHTENMENT HERO

THE OCEAN MAY BE HIS GRAVE, BUT THE WHOLE GLOBE IS
HIS MONUMENT

Cook's killing on a remote shore was recognised in Europe
as an event at once shocking and momentous, and in death
the explorer was accorded tributes he had never known in
life. Only with the publication of his journal of the second
voyage in 1777 – almost a year after Cook sailed on his last
voyage – had his remarkable qualities been fully revealed to
the reading public. The first voyage was more Banks's than
Cook's in the public eye, and the botanist's amorous exploits
in Tahiti rather than the discoveries of the voyage filled the
pages of the newspapers and periodicals. Even the achievements of the magnificent second voyage were blurred for
a time. Cook's report to the Admiralty when he reached
the Cape of Good Hope in March 1775 on his way home
covered only the final year of the voyage, since he assumed
that when Captain Tobias Furneaux on the consort vessel the
Adventure reached England he would have reported on the
explorations carried out before the two ships lost company
with each other off New Zealand in October 1773. Inexplicably, Furneaux seems to have said little on this aspect of
the voyage. His letter to the Admiralty from the Cape in
April 1774 took up most space describing the grisly episode

in which a boat's crew from the *Adventure* was killed and eaten at Grass Cove, New Zealand. Furneaux arrived back in England in July 1774, a full year before Cook, but seems never to have reported in writing on the voyage to the Admiralty, other than handing in his journal. Both he and the newspapers of the day were most interested in the Grass Cove massacre, and the bringing to England of the Society Islander, Omai (Mai).

It was left to an unnamed lieutenant of the *Resolution* to alert the public at home that Cook's second voyage had been extraordinary in more ways than one. His letter from the Cape was printed in *Lloyd's Evening Post* for 30 June–3 July 1775. It made much of the fact that the crew had been 'amazingly healthful', losing not a single man to scurvy, and that in the search for a southern continent the *Resolution* had sailed through 'islands of ice' as far south as latitude 71° S. The expedition had 'discovered no Continent, but the ice is a plain indication of more land, though not seen by us'. Cook himself was back by late July, with his own journals and reports to hand in to the Admiralty. Within two weeks of his return Cook was presented to the King, and promoted Post Captain (for a naval officer a key promotion, since if he lived long enough, in time he would become an admiral). In the months that followed Cook was elected Fellow of the Royal Society and there were other forms of recognition too. He was painted by Nathaniel Dance, and Boswell recorded a pleasant meeting with him. In his own professional circles Cook was on easy terms with the Earl of Sandwich, First Lord of the Admiralty, and with other members of the Board of Admiralty. It took longer for recognition to spread more widely. The first newspaper reports of his voyage were sketchy and confused, and again most attention centred on the fate of the

8. *The Wedgwood medallion of Captain Cook, white on blue jasper, 1777, here in an elaborate wooden frame. Made by Josiah Wedgwood as part of his series of 'illustrious moderns', the Cook medallion would have taken its place among the 52 'Statesmen and Commanders' of the series; other categories included philosophers (30) and English poets (24).*

Adventure's boat crew. A report in the *Lloyd's Evening Post* for 7–10 August 1775, which seems to have been based on a conversation with Cook, was correct in establishing his furthest position south at latitude 73° 30' S, but carelessly wrong in saying that there he turned back from 'an amazing face of perpendicular rock' instead of a mass of Antarctic ice.

The publication of Cook's own account of *A Voyage towards the South Pole, and Round the World* in 1777 brought a different emphasis. There was still much in the reviews of the book about Omai, Tahiti, and the Grass Cove killings,

but also visible was the outline of a new kind of hero, commemorated earlier in the year when Josiah Wedgwood
issued a medallion of Cook as part of his series of 'illustrious moderns'. The last sentence of Cook's journal as he
anchored at Spithead put what was for contemporaries the
most astounding aspect of the voyage briefly and bluntly;
'Having been absent from England Three Years and Eight-
een Days, in which time I lost but four men and only one of
them by sickness.' In the published account either Cook or
his editor, Dr Douglas, elaborated on the achievement:

> Our having discovered the possibility of preserving
> health amongst a numerous ship's company, for such a
> length of time, in such varieties of climate, and amidst
> such continued hardships and fatigues, will make this
> Voyage remarkable in the opinion of every benevolent
> person, when the disputes about a Southern Continent
> shall have ceased to engage the attention and to divide
> the judgement of philosophers.

This concluded a four-page summary of the methods Cook
used to combat scurvy, another version of which he put into
the form of a paper to the Royal Society, 'A Discourse upon
some late improvements of the means for preserving the
health of mariners'. Cook had left on his third voyage by the
time this was presented to the Society, so it was read by Sir
John Pringle, President of the Society, on 30 November 1776,
when he also awarded Cook, *in absentia*, the Society's Copley
Gold Medal. It was given, Pringle said, to one who 'per-
petuates the means by which Britain may now, on the most
distant voyages, preserve numbers of her intrepid sons, her
Mariners'. He contrasted Cook's record on his second voyage

with the dismal totals of losses on earlier voyages, Anson's in particular (when out of 1,900 men who sailed almost 1,400 sickened and died). He concluded his oration with a summary of Cook's achievements that was repeated in the more accessible pages of the *Gentleman's Magazine*. This printed a summary of Cook's 'Method taken for preserving the Health of the Crew', and concluded:

> As a navigator Captain Cook undoubtedly ranks as the first of this or any age of nation, and to every other requisite seems to have added that humanity in which seamen and discoverers, especially of former times, have been too generally and shockingly deficient. Not a gun, as it appears, was ever wantonly or unnecessarily fired *by his order* ... and his attention to the health of his own mariners was so singularly successful, that ... he lost only one man by sickness ... how meritorious must that person appear, who hath ... not only discovered, but surveyed, vast tracts of new coasts, who hath dispelled the illusion of a *terra australis incognita*, fixed the bounds of the habitable earth, as well as those of the navigable ocean in the southern hemisphere!

When the first brief reports of Cook's death reached England in January 1780 the account of his second voyage, just issued in its third edition, was scoured for information as obituary writers reminded readers of what they had lost. The first obituaries appeared in London newspapers within days of news of his death reaching England. The *Morning Chronicle* of 14 January 1780 set the tone when it lamented that Cook's 'murder' was 'not only a national loss, but a misfortune in which all Europe must feel itself deeply interested'. A few days later the same newspaper printed a paean of praise by a contributor, 'Columbus', who claimed to have known Cook personally. The figure of the hero was now more firmly drawn. He was of humble origins, a man whose technical skills were matched by his humanity, whose care for his crew was shown in his attention to their health, and who in the end sacrificed himself in his concern for their safety. Cook's record as 'a discoverer of unknown countries' began with his youth in the coal trade:

> Taught by his early education to sail always near the shore … he was never afraid of approaching an unknown coast, and would for weeks and months together persevere to sail along sands and shoals, the very appearance of which would have been thought by most seamen a sufficient reason for leaving them.

This insight was followed by a listing of Cook's strengths: his courage, knowledge of hydrography and astronomy, emphasis on shipboard health ('nothing of which he trusted to any one but himself'), the humanity with which he treated natives, and 'his attention to the safety of those under his command, and his fixed resolution that no one should incur more danger than himself'. It was this determination, the writer concluded, that probably led to his death. A similar point was made in the *Gentleman's Magazine* for January which, echoing its earlier review of Cook's second voyage, asserted that, 'Capt. Cook was on the defensive, and in this, as a voyager, was almost singular, that he never knowingly injured, but always studied to benefit the savages whom he visited.'

In Britain the time was right for a less conventional hero

than the military figures of the past. The War of American Independence was dragging to a close, but the colonies had been lost; the Navy was rent by political quarrels; and growing doubts were being expressed about British activities in India. The concept of a hero devoted to the arts of peace rather than war was reflected in the poetic responses to Cook's death. Among the first was Anna Seward's 'Elegy on Captain Cook', first published in June 1780, and widely reprinted in the periodicals. With little information as yet available about the last voyage, Seward turned to the account of the second voyage as she depicted Cook, 'the mild Hero', sailing to the Pacific islands as the emissary of 'HUMANITY', carrying livestock and plants, and preaching the gospel of peace. Cook was 'BENEVOLENCE' personified, but he was killed by those he tried to help, and 'His bones now whiten an accursed shore.' The poem was, the *Gentleman's Magazine* judged, 'worthy of the memory of one of the greatest men this or any age of nation has produced'.

The authorised account of Cook's last voyage began with a two-page eulogy by an unnamed naval officer (Admiral of the Fleet, John Forbes, it later transpired) explaining how Cook 'raised himself, solely by his merits, from a very obscure birth, to the rank of Post Captain in the royal navy'. There was no mention here of the role of those influential patrons who recognised, and eased the way for, Cook's talents. In carefully-weighted phrases Cook's virtues as a navigator were catalogued, and the health record of his second voyage again singled out for special praise. 'He was father to his people,' the eulogy concluded, 'who were attached to him by affection, and obedient from confidence.' There is a reminder here of the heartfelt tribute of Heinrich Zimmermann, Able Seaman on the *Resolution*, who wrote of the scene at Kealakekua Bay, 'Everyone in the ships was stricken dumb, crushed, and felt as though he had lost his father.'

Mention of Zimmermann is a reminder that Cook's voyages had a European dimension in more ways than one. Solander and Spöring on the first voyage, the Forsters and Sparrman on the second, all sailed as supernumeraries with Cook. The accounts of the voyages were translated into a half-dozen European languages. The natural history specimens and 'artificial curiosities' (ethnographic items) brought back by Cook's crews found their way into museums in St Petersburg, Berne, Vienna, Florence and Göttingen. In the years before the French Revolution changed everything writers across Europe produced eulogies of Cook, praising him as a standard-bearer of the Enlightenment. As the writer of an anonymous account of his third voyage put it, 'The ocean may be his grave. But the whole globe is his monument.' Much was made of the order by the French government after the outbreak of war in 1778 that Cook's ships should be given a safe conduct. This example was followed by Benjamin Franklin on behalf of Congress since Cook and his crews, 'common Friends to Mankind', were engaged in

an Undertaking truly laudable in itself, as the Increase of Geographical Knowledge facilitates the Communication between distant Nations, in the Exchange of useful Products and Manufactures, and the Extension of the Arts, whereby the common Enjoyments of human life are multiply'd and augmented.

The Spanish government, it is true, was less accommodating. Nervous about British ambitions in the North Pacific, it sent instructions to its officials in Mexico to detain Cook and his crews if his ships called at a Spanish port.

Even before the end of the war with France in 1783, a French diplomat engaged in the repatriation of prisoners of war asked the Admiralty for details of Cook's life since French academicians wished to honour him. Abbé Delille's poem, 'Les Jardins' (published in France in 1782, and then translated into English), set out the difference between Cook and previous discoverers:

> To foreign climes and rude, where nought before
> Announc'd our vessels but their cannons' roar
> For other gifts thy better mind decreed,
> The sheep, the heifer, and the stately steed;
> The plough, and all thy country's arts; the crimes
> Atoning thus of earlier savage times.
> With peace each land thy bark was wont to hail,
> And tears and blessings fill'd thy parting sail.

This was pushing Cook's virtues a little too far – cannon, muskets and the lash might be last resorts, but he would turn to them if the occasion demanded. A few years later Pierre Lemontey's prize-winning 'Éloge de Jacques Cook' (one of twenty essays on Cook submitted to the Academy of Marseilles) followed the same theme when it portrayed him as 'representing the best in a European civilization in the process of renouncing its murderous, barbaric practices when confronted with the native inhabitants of regions'. For Lemontey, who came from a merchant family, Cook's discoveries promised a new kind of global commerce between Europe and the South Seas, based on mutual benefit rather than force.

Other essayists saw Cook's life as evidence of how in England, unlike in the France of the *ancien régime*, a man of humble background could rise in his profession. Once in the Pacific, his behaviour towards its peoples was exemplary. He set a personal example (not much followed by his crews, it is true) in resisting the charms of Polynesian women, and strove to protect the islanders from the twin evils of venereal disease and alcohol. He refused to become entangled in local disputes and wars, and was even-handed in his distribution of gifts. Above all, he made a genuine attempt to understand the customs of the peoples he encountered, and he refused to pass judgement on them. An endearing indication of the spread of Cook's reputation through Europe came in the recollection of the Austrian playwright, poet and essayist, Franz Grillparzer (born in 1791) of how when he was a boy

> there was a collection of travel books of which the story of Captain Cook's circumnavigation especially fascinated me so that I was soon more at home in Otahiti than in our own house.

In Italy the Royal Academy of Florence published in 1785, in Italian and English, an elegy by Michelangiolo Gianetti to show that 'it delights in giving due honour to Heroes, wherever they may be found'. For Gianetti the virtues shown by Cook were

> more worthy to be celebrated, than the victorious prowess of military Chiefs, for he was 'A Hero', at once sailor, warrior and philosopher, who displayed the qualities of magnanimity, enterprise and tranquillity.

The elegy picked up what was now becoming a common feature of the tributes to Cook, his beginnings as

> a common sailor on board a merchant ship ... A proud line of ancestors, the imposing lustre of titles, and immense riches, are not necessary to make a man truly great; For Cook enjoyed no such advantages.

Almost without exception, the obituaries and eulogies praised Cook for introducing to the peoples of the Pacific the useful arts of Europe – from new plants and strains of cattle to the latest technology and commercial skills. And, as Bernard Smith has pointed out, the hero stood alone; there is no acknowledgement in these literary tributes of the part played in Cook's voyages by his fellow officers and his civilian scientific companions.

COOK, EVER HONOUR'D, IMMORTAL SHALL LIVE

A significant part in the heroising process was played by the artist John Webber, who soon after his return to England in 1780 produced two paintings of the death of Cook, an oil and a watercolour. As far as we know, Webber was not in either of the two boats that took Cook to the beach at Kealakekua Bay on the morning of 14th February, and he seems not to have made a drawing of the scene at the time (certainly there was no sketch of the death of Cook among the drawings he handed in to the Admiralty on the *Resolution*'s return). The paintings of a crowded and chaotic scene show Cook, his back to his attackers, gesturing to the boats to stop firing as he is about to be struck down. In January 1784, six months before the publication of the authorised account, an engraving by

9. 'The Death of Captain Cook' by John Webber, 1784; engraving by Francesco Bartolozzi (figures) and William Byrne (landscape). This famous print follows closely Webber's oil painting (see dust-jacket) except that it shows Cook dressed in white (as in Webber's watercolour of the scene). He is thus illuminated as in a spot-light, against the dark background of his attackers and the trees.

Francesco Bartolozzi and William Byrne based on Webber's watercolour was published in London (earlier impressions exist dated 1782 and 1783). Its title ran: 'The Death of Captain Cook...by the murdering Dagger of a Barbarian at Carakakooa ... He having there become a Victim to his own Humanity.' Doubts as to whether Webber perhaps intended to show Cook beckoning the boats to come closer in rather than ordering them to stop firing have been resolved by the recent discovery of a printed explanation (almost certainly by Webber) that the engraving shows Cook 'calling to his People, in the Boats to cease Firing'. Unlike the prone figure of Rickman's account, Webber's Cook stands tall and upright, musket in hand, making a choice between war and peace at the cost of his own life. The engraving took its place alongside the best-selling prints based on Benjamin West's earlier painting of the death of Wolfe at Quebec and his celebrated later painting of the death of Nelson on the quarter-deck of the *Victory*. Like Webber's painting, West's were intended as a moving tribute to a dying hero rather than an accurate depiction of the death scene. West explained his attitude when criticising a rival painting that showed Nelson dying, as he actually did, in the bloody shambles of the ship's noisome orlop deck:

> Wolfe must not die like a common soldier under a Bush, neither should Nelson be represented dying in the gloomy hold of a ship, like a sick man in a Prison Hole.

Presumably because of its prior publication, the Bartolozzi engraving was not issued in the authorised account, which therefore failed to include among its many plates any illustration of the death of the book's hero. This omission became a major selling point for an abridged edition of Cook's voyages in four octavo volumes published by Stockdale later in 1784. It included an engraving of the death of Cook, drawn by the artist D.P. Dodd and 'others who where [sic] on the Spot'. An accompanying note pointed out that since no view of Cook's death had appeared in the quarto edition and 'as so interesting a subject will tend to gratify the curiosity of the reader, uncommon diligence has been exerted to procure a masterly representation of so affecting a catastrophe.' Whether any eye-witness of the scene on the beach was in fact involved in Dodd's drawing is open to doubt, but what is striking is its contrast to Webber's depiction. Cook, disarmed and hatless, is shown lying flat on his face at the water's edge, a helpless victim surrounded by exultant islanders.

The engraving based on the watercolour by Webber, the official artist on the voyage, became the standard version of

10. 'The Death of Captain James Cook' by D.P. Dodd, 1784. A notably unheroic depiction, with a helpless and prone Cook either being pushed into the sea or being dragged back towards his attackers, one of whom seems to be trying to pacify the others.

the death of Cook. A possible example of its influence can be seen in the intriguing story of the hitherto unknown painting by John Cleveley of the death of Cook. John Cleveley was a professional painter whose brother, James, was carpenter on the *Resolution*. During the voyage James made several drawings of Pacific scenes that served as the basis for paintings by John after the return of the ships and, in 1788, for a series of engravings. The best-known engraving is a panorama of Kealakekua Bay, with Cook in the foreground drawn in a Webber-like posture, apparently beckoning to the boats to stop firing. The assumption that the central scene in the engraving was copied from the painting has now been

11. *The death of Captain Cook, oil painting by George Carter, 1781. Another
painting, not much copied, of Cook facing his attackers. If the dating
is correct, Carter's painting seems to be a direct challenge to Webber's
interpretation of the scene. Not all viewers were enamoured of Carter's
effort. The* Public Advertiser *commented that 'The chief Figure bears
a stronger Resemblance to the hero of a Porridge-pot, than to our great
Navigator round the World.'*

thrown into doubt. In 2004 four previously unknown watercolours of Pacific scenes by John Cleveley went on sale, with
contemporary labels stating that he had painted them from
sketches drawn by his brother. All interest has focused on
the painting showing the death of Cook, for unlike the later
engraving it shows an enraged Cook swinging the butt of
his musket at his attackers. It was not the first representation
to show something like this, for George Carter's oil painting of 1781 also showed Cook facing his assailants, but in
a more defensive mode. There is an energy and fury about
Cleveley's painting absent from Carter's, and quite at odds
with Webber's self-sacrificial hero.

12. *The death of Captain Cook by John Cleveley, 1788 engraving. An even more crowded and frenzied scene than that depicted by Webber, but the essentials are the same, except that here Cook is picked out by the white puffs of musket-smoke that (as Bernard Smith has observed) seem to form a halo around him.*

We know that James Cleveley was not an eye-witness of the death of Cook since he was in one of the boats patrolling the southeast side of Kealakekua Bay. His depiction is not necessarily a contradiction of the scene as painted by Webber; for we could be looking at slightly different stages of the fracas, as described by Thomas Edgar, Master of the *Discovery*:

A Man came behind him and knocked him down with a club on his knees he immediately got up and rashly went strong into the middle of the crowd following the man who he beat with the butt end of his piece. He returned down again and was close to the water ...

13. *The death of Captain Cook, watercolour by John Cleveley, c. 1780.*
This is the central scene in Cleveley's recently-discovered panoramic
painting of Kealakekua Bay on 14 February 1779. It shows an aggressive
Cook, backed by his marines, turning on his attackers. In the left foreground
the recumbent figure appears to be a marine, being attacked by a club-
wielding islander.

He was then stabbed, knocked into the sea, and finished off
with rocks. In Cleveley, Cook has turned on his assailants;
in Webber, a retreating Cook has his back to the crowd as
he signals to the boats. What is of interest is not only the
different moment in time shown by the two artists, but also
the decision by the engraver of 1788 (John Cleveley could
not have been responsible since he died in 1786) to change
the representation of an aggressive Cook to conform with
the now familiar interpretation by Webber. It is perhaps an
eighteenth-century example of political correctness.

   The magnificent engravings in the authorised account,
showing locations from Alaska to New Zealand, also

conveyed the message of Cook as a man of peace. Webber was careful to select scenes of greetings, ceremonies and exchanges. Stone-throwing, jeering crowds, musket and cannon fire, burning canoes and huts, were little in evidence. Webber's role in interpreting Cook continued after the publication of the official account, for he served as consultant to the popular pantomime produced by Philippe Jacques de Loutherbourg, with libretto by John O'Keefe, *Omai, or, a Trip round the World*. This opened at Covent Garden in December 1785, was revived several times in the following years, and during its various runs was seen by audiences totalling many tens of thousands.

Four years later a 'Grand Serious-Pantomimic-Ballet', *The Death of Captain Cook*, opened at Covent Garden with separate productions in several provincial cities. With music only, it was a version of a French pantomime, *La Mort du Capitaine Cook*, first performed in Paris in 1788. It bore little resemblance to reality, but its spectacular settings caught the imagination of the theatre-going public. Its depiction of Cook as a tragic hero caught the imagination of the painter Johann Zoffany, who at one time had hoped to sail on Cook's second voyage. His painting, 'The Death of Cook', probably begun in the early 1790s but left unfinished, looked back to classical times, with the feather headgear of the Hawaiians resembling the helmets of ancient Greek warriors. For those who wanted to see the real thing, the Leverian Museum in London included a Sandwich Room, dedicated 'To the Immortal Memory of Captain Cook', filled with exhibits brought back from the third voyage. These included 'the superb cloak taken by the king of Owhyee [Hawai'i] from his own shoulders, and by him placed on the shoulders of Capt. Cook' in January 1779.

The costumes of de Loutherbourg's *Omai* were praised by many reviewers. By contrast, the plot found little favour, but O'Keefe's libretto, in which Molesworth Phillips may have had a hand, made some serious points. In a mix of personalities and events from the three voyages, Cook appears as a peace-loving hero who spread the gospel of the Enlightenment. As Britannia explained to the 'Queen of the Isles' (Tahiti), unlike Alexander the Great who also travelled round the world but brought only death, Cook 'taught mankind how to *live*'. An English sea-captain sang:

> He came, and he saw, not to conquer but save;
> The Caesar of Britain was he;
> Who scorn'd the ambition of making a slave
> While Britons themselves are so free.
> Now the Genius of Britain forbids us to grieve,
> Since Cook, ever honour'd, immortal shall live.

At this the pantomime finished with the lowering of a huge painted backcloth, 'The Apotheosis of Captain Cook', issued as an engraving by de Loutherbourg in 1794. Cook is shown being drawn up above the smoke and fury of Kealakekua Bay amid clouds of glory, holding in his hand not the conventional sword, but a sextant. It was the visual representation of those literary responses that celebrated Cook as a new kind of British hero.

If the pantomime was for the most part a celebration of a peaceful, freedom-loving Cook, a more disturbing note was sounded in the final scene in an exchange between the sea-captain and a chorus of 'Indians':

14. 'The Apotheosis of Captain Cook' by Philippe de Loutherbourg and John
Webber, 1794 engraving.

CAPTAIN: Ally of Joy! Owhyee's fatal shore
            Brave Cook, your great Orono is no more.
INDIANS: Mourn, Owhyee's fatal shore
            For Cook, our great Orono, is no more.

By both English and Hawaiians, Cook is acknowledged as the 'great Orono', the name that appeared, first in Ledyard and then in Douglas. A footnote in the printed text scuffed over the issue with the explanation that 'Orono' was 'a Demi-God, or hero, and the distinguished title with which the natives honoured Captain Cook'. Amid the colourful costumes and scenery of de Loutherbourg's production it is doubtful whether textual subtleties were noticed by many playgoers, but there was no getting away from the fact that O'Keefe had observed that during the stay in Hawai'i Cook, willingly or otherwise, had been treated as a god.

One of the most telling examples of the new concern came from William Cowper, whose poem on Cook, 'Charity', written soon after news of the explorer's death reached England, is remembered for its famous couplet:

While Cook is loved for savage lives he saved,
See Cortez odious for a world enslaved!

However, the poet's reading of the authorised account of the voyage produced a change of tone as he recoiled from the realisation that Cook had been 'content to be worshipped', and so had incurred 'the guilt of sacrilege'. 'God is a jealous God,' Cowper remarked, as he went on to argue that Cook's acceptance of his worship as Lono had resulted in the withdrawal of 'the remarkable interposition of Providence in his favour', and so led to his death. In Germany Goethe took up the theme when he commented that the death of Cook was 'a great catalogue of a great life', but that 'a man who is deified cannot live longer, and must not live longer for his own and for other people's sake'.

Away from the Lono issue, some readers of the authorised account were not impressed by the personality of Cook as presented by Douglas and King. A fellow officer, Captain Edward Thompson, thought the official account did scant justice to Charles Clerke. In a cryptic entry in his diary, he wrote, whether from personal knowledge or not is unclear, 'Of Cook, more is said than he merits. Of Clerke, less than he deserves ... Cook was the better Sailor – but Clerke was the better Man.' When Samwell published his *Narrative of the Death of Captain James Cook* in 1786 he was at pains to explain in the preface that he had written it because 'public opinion seemed to attribute the loss of Captain Cook's life, in some measure, to rashness and too much confidence on his side; whereas nothing can be more ill-founded and unjust.'

The process of elevating Cook the hero was continued by the publication in 1788 of Andrew Kippis's *Life of Captain James Cook*. Kippis, editor of *Biographia Britannica*, was a Nonconformist minister and a professional writer. The book was less a biography of Cook than a summary of his voyages, although it included tributes from King, Johann Reinhold Forster and others, and a selection of elegies and poems written in the explorer's honour. With the anti-slave trade and anti-slavery campaign gaining momentum, it is not surprising that these included pieces written by those prominent in the burgeoning humanitarian movement. So in her 'Black Slave Trade', printed in Kippis, Hannah More lamented:

Had these possess'd, O Cook! Thy gentle mind,
Thy love of arts, thy love of humankind;
Had these pursued thy mild and liberal plan,
Discoverers had not been a curse to man!

The *Gentleman's Magazine* thought Kippis's 'compilation' was simply an abridgement of the published narratives of Cook's voyages. 'We have here Dr Hawkesworth [editor of Cook's first voyage] over again, Captain Cook over again, Dr John Douglas over again ...' Even so, Kippis's two-volume work remained in print for a hundred years, and during that time became – if only by default – the standard biography of Cook. At least forty-eight editions of the book have been traced (up to 1925), and despite the accusation of repetition its description of Cook's death was based, not on the version in Douglas, but on David Samwell's account of 1786. It is true that where Kippis allowed himself editorial comment he followed the line of Douglas and other commentators. Once again, readers were reminded of the difference between Cook's voyages and those of the rapacious Spaniards of a bygone age. Cook's intention was 'not to enlarge private dominion, but to promote general knowledge; the new tribes of earth were visited as friends.' Much was made of Cook's introduction of livestock and plants to the Pacific islands, but as befitted a minister of religion Kippis set his sights higher:

Perhaps, our late voyages may be the means appointed by Providence, of spreading, in due time, the blessings of civilization among the numerous tribes of the South Pacific Ocean ... Nothing can more effectually contribute to the attainment of this great end, than a wise and rational introduction of the Christian religion.

There was another side to the worldwide explorations that Cook personified, as even as staunch an admirer as Kippis admitted when he wrote that the issue of the effects of the voyages on the discovered was 'not wholly free from doubts and difficulties'. This was an acknowledgement that there existed a foreboding not only about earlier discovery voyages but also even about those of Cook and his contemporaries. A reader of the 'entertaining narrative' of Cook's first voyage complained to the *Gentleman's Magazine*: 'It gives me pain to find my countrymen ... exercising on the harmless Indians [sic] a spirit peculiar, as we hoped, to Spanish invaders.' George Forster, in his personal record of Cook's second voyage, had famously asked whether it would not have been 'better for the discoverers and the discovered, that the South Seas had still remained unknown to Europe and its restless inhabitants'. Horace Walpole had already written in similar terms when he said of Tahiti that 'not even that little speck could escape European restlessness'. It was an apprehension that Cook himself shared. In a journal entry at Queen Charlotte Sound, New Zealand, he lamented that

> we debouch their Morals already too prone to vice and we interduce along them wants and diseases which they never knew before and which serves only to disturb that happy tranquillity they and their fore Fathers had injoy'd.

In France the Abbé Raynal and Denis Diderot in their influential *Histoire philosophique et politique des Indes* were expressing opinions that a later age would call anticolonial; while James Dunbar wrote in 1780 that discovery voyages have never yet been happy for any of the tribes of mankind visited by us ... the natives of that happy island [Tahiti], so cruelly abused, will have cause to lament for ages, that any European vessel ever touched their shores.

Within days of the news of Cook's death reaching England, a contributor wrote to the *Morning Chronicle* in strikingly different terms from the customary tributes that were filling the broadsheets:

We call Cook, most justly, a civilizer, a circumnavigator, a great man. Had we been born in an island in the South-Seas, we should perhaps have called him an invader, a pirate ... Were a body of strange beings, with strange arms and a strange language to land at Plymouth, we should ... kill them unless they went away.

By the time that Douglas's edition of Cook's last voyage was published in 1784 this was an attitude that had to be countered. In an otherwise conventional epic poem, 'The Cave of Neptune', which praised the deeds of the Navy in the recent war, the poet took a side swipe at Cook:

Return contented to your native shore
Nor rashly distant regions here explore:
Rest with your own – nor seek further climes
To bear your standard, and receive your crimes.

In case this was not clear enough, a note added: 'If any islands yet remain undiscovered, the author of this poem hopes they will continue so; or, at least, until the morals of Europe are changed for the better.' To rebut such sentiments the *Critical Review* adopted what was becoming a standard response to arguments that sprang from 'an affected humanity'. It admitted that the Pacific islanders had not always benefited from the visits of Cook and other British navigators, but this it ascribed to 'their ignorance and inattention than to his neglect'. The debate had begun.

YOU MEN OF CAPTAIN COOK; YOU RISE UPON US IN EVERY TRIAL

Away from the effusions of literary figures and discussions in fashionable salons, seafaring men had their own view of Cook, one of admiration for his skills as a navigator and hydrographer. To his command of a grand sweep of exploration on an oceanic scale was allied an unrelenting insistence on accuracy. One of the most surprising tributes came from George Forster, who had accompanied his father Johann Reinhold Forster on Cook's second voyage, and who had witnessed the shipboard discord between the two men. In 1787 the younger Forster wrote 'Cook, der Entdecker' ('Cook, the Discoverer'), a 20,000-word introduction to his translation into German of the official account of Cook's third voyage. At one level Forster's piece was a summary of the geographical achievement of Cook's three voyages; at another it was an awed recollection of the dominant personality of the navigator. Even as a landsman Forster noticed that when Cook came on deck he would often note slackness in a rope or line that the officer on watch had overlooked. When the officers were reckoning distance by eye it was usually Cook's estimate that was correct. His handling of his officers and men, his attention to health on his ships, and his sense of when discipline must be rigidly enforced and when it might be relaxed, were all admired by Forster. Above all, he was impressed by Cook's 'iron perseverance', which enabled him to transform the map of the Pacific, so that 'he remains, as a mariner and discoverer, incomparable and unique'.

As early as his first voyage, the relatively unknown Lieutenant Cook wrote of his chart of the North Island of New Zealand, 'I believe that this Island will never be found to differ materially from the figure I have given it.' There is a sense of permanence here, of posterity even, of the triumph of human willpower aided by science over nature in all its forms. The 'impediments' (to use one of Cook's favourite words) of ice, fog, tempest and reef were treated with a seaman's respect but were not allowed to distract from the obsessive determination to survey and describe. As Boswell wrote, the explorer had 'a ballance in his mind for truth as nice as scales for weighing a guinea'. A new dimension had emerged in British seaborne endeavour, and Cook's voyages became a template for those who followed. Long after Cook died, navigators were using his charts – his own men, of course, but also those who had never sailed with him, had never known him. So respectful was Captain Robert Fitzroy of *Beagle* fame that sixty years after the explorer's death he insisted on referring to Tahiti as 'Otaheite', because 'our immortal countryman, Cook, wrote Otaheite, and it is difficult to hear or see the word without thinking of him.'

For those who sailed with him, Cook was not always the beloved commander of the conventional biographies, which are perhaps unduly influenced by the emotional reactions of the crew to his death. It would be surprising if on the long, arduous voyages there were no tensions on board, but apart from the running disputes on the second voyage with Johann

Reinhold Forster the journals are studiously silent about these. Indeed, when Cook compiled the published version of that voyage he took out critical references in his manuscript journal to his officers that in retrospect he decided were unfair. On the *Endeavour* voyage, if the recollections of Dr Solander (Joseph Banks's assistant) are to be trusted, Cook was 'jealous' of John Gore (Third and then Second Lieutenant), who held 'a sort of separate command in the vessel', supervising transactions with the islanders and on occasion defying Cook's orders. There might be something in this, for Gore had sailed with both Byron and Wallis, and as far as Pacific voyaging was concerned was at that time vastly more experienced than Cook. Yet Cook took Gore on the *Resolution* as his First Lieutenant on the third voyage, and although the two men did not always see eye to eye on the exploration of the Alaskan coast it is difficult to accept Solander's earlier verdict that 'they hate each other'. The real problem officer on the third voyage was John Williamson, Third Lieutenant of the *Resolution*, who figures in some of the most controversial incidents of the voyage. Cook's anger at what he saw as the unnecessary shooting by Williamson of a Hawaiian at Kauai in January 1778 led to the lieutenant asking Cook, quite improperly, not to send him on such duties again. Williamson was critical of Cook's behaviour at a sacred ceremony on Tonga, and furious when Cook seemed not to take seriously the theft of his gun, although, Williamson complained, 'if a small nail was stolen from Captn Cook, the thief if taken was most severely punished'. His behaviour while in charge of the launch on the morning of Cook's death was vehemently criticised by his shipmates and seems to have led to a duel with Lieutenant Molesworth Phillips. In Midshipman James Trevenen's words, he was 'a wretch, feared

& hated by his inferiors, detested by his equals, and despised by his superiors'. Then there was Bligh, the youthful Master of the *Resolution*, who is rarely mentioned by Cook, but who seems already to be showing some of those characteristics that were to make him notorious in his later career. Marginal notes he wrote on his copy of the published account of the voyage show a particular dislike of James King, who he alleged always feigned illness whenever a dangerous situation needed attention, and who was incapable of bearing any hardship.

Of Cook's behaviour we catch a few glimpses, although understandably not in the official journals. In his account of the voyage Heinrich Zimmermann gave his impressions of Cook, not all from first-hand observation since as a mere seaman he would not have had access to the great cabin:

> Captain Cook was a tall, handsome man, of somewhat spare build, slightly bent but strong, dark brown in complexion and stern of visage ... He was very strict and hot tempered, so much so that the slightest insubordination of an officer or sailor upset him completely. He was unyielding where the ship's rules and the punishment inflicted for breaches of the same were concerned ... Perhaps no sea officer has ever had such supreme authority over the officers serving under him as he, so that not one of them dared to contradict him. He would often sit at the table with his officers without saying a word, and was always very reserved.

In a much-quoted passage Zimmermann went on to reflect that Cook 'was born to deal with savages and he was never happier than in association with them', although if thwarted

15. *Engraving by Francesco Bartolozzi of John Webber's portrait of Captain Cook, 1784, showing him, in Heinrich Zimmermann's words, 'stern of visage'.*

by them 'he burned with rage'. A telling description of Cook in such a rage comes from Trevenen, who had been upbraided by Cook for some minor misdemeanour:

> Of course I had a *heiva* of the old man ... *Heiva* the name of the dances of the Southern [New Zealand] Islanders, which bore so great a resemblance to the violent motions

and stampings on the Deck of Captn Cooke in the parox-
ysms of passion, into which he often threw himself upon
the slightest occasion that they were universally known
by the same name, & it was a common saying amongst
both officers & people 'The old boy has been tipping a
heiva to such or such a one'.

A tongue-lashing for neglectful officers became something
altogether more physical for delinquent seamen. As on any
Royal Navy ship, flogging was used as a routine punishment
by Cook. On the third voyage there was a marked increase in
the number of floggings on the *Resolution*. As far as we can
judge, those flogged accepted their punishment as an ines-
capable part of life in the Navy, but it is clear that as the third
voyage progressed there was increasing discontent among
the crew over other issues. Cook's failure to avenge the
killing of the *Adventure*'s boat crew when he had one of the
Maori leaders responsible in his power at Queen Charlotte's
Sound in February 1777 seems to have stirred deep resent-
ment, especially as the crew were on short rations at this time
as a punishment for unexplained thefts of provisions. King
wrote that there was 'an appearance of general disobedience
among the people', while Cook accused the crew of 'a very
mutinous proceeding'. Cook was even more forthright when
in December 1778 off Maui his crew wrote him a letter com-
plaining about the replacement of grog by a sugar-cane con-
coction. Cook's reaction to this unusual step by the crew was
to accuse them of being 'mutinous' and 'turbulent'. Mutiny,
with its mandatory death penalty, was not an accusation to
be taken lightly by the crew, and Cook's follow-up threat that
'in future they might not expect the least indulgence from
him' was less frightening than some alternatives.

It is important to keep such troubles in perspective. Some captains on long voyages ran into problems that make Cook's seem insignificant, On his voyage to New Holland in the *Roebuck* in 1699 William Dampier put his First Lieutenant in irons, and slept on the quarter-deck with firearms by his side, 'it scarce being safe for me to lie in my Cabbin, by Reasons of the Discontents among my Men'. A few years later Woodes Rogers' circumnavigation was so afflicted by dissensions and death threats that on his return Rogers pleaded with the owners, 'For Christs Sake don't let me be torn to pieces at home after I have been so rackt abroad.' Dampier was a former buccaneer ('that Old Pyrateing Dog' in his lieutenant's words), and Rogers a privateer; but regular Navy captains on the much-lauded Arctic voyages of the nineteenth century sometimes set miserable examples in terms of management of their officers and men. Edward Belcher and Richard Collinson both returned to England with furious officers confined to their cabins and under threat of court martial.

Cook's journals, his charts, and the men who had sailed with him dominated the burgeoning British activity in the Pacific in the decades after his death. In his introduction to the authorised account of the third voyage Dr Douglas insisted that Britain, 'whose commerce is boundless, must take the lead in reaping the full advantage of her own discoveries'. In 1787 a fleet sailed for Cook's landing place in New South Wales, Botany Bay, to establish the first European settlement in Australia. Were it not for Cook's unassailable reputation, his report of a single brief visit to Botany Bay might have been regarded as too slight a basis on which to risk sending 1,300 people to the other side of the world without further investigation. By this time the Greenland whale fishery could not meet the growing domestic and industrial demand for oil, and Cook's charts encouraged dozens of British and American whalers to sail to far-southerly latitudes in pursuit of the sperm whale. Far away in the North Pacific Cook's men had drawn attention to the ease with which sea-otter pelts and seal skins could be obtained along the coast from Nootka Sound to Alaska. In the authorised account of the voyage Captain King noted that prime sea-otter pelts, traded for a handful of beads on the northwest coast, fetched 120 dollars at Canton. By the mid-1780s British merchants in India and China were fitting out vessels for the coast, and others from Europe and the United States soon followed. It was, a later writer declared, as if a new gold coast had been discovered.

Prominent in these ventures was Sir Joseph Banks. The young botanist who had sailed with Cook on the *Endeavour* had become one of the most influential men in England – President of the Royal Society, patron of the sciences, adviser of cabinet ministers, and promoter of enterprises associated with Cook's discoveries. Banks was, King wrote, 'the common centre of we discoverers', and after Cook's death he became the self-appointed guardian of his reputation. This was not an onerous task, for criticisms of Cook as an explorer were few and far between. His failure in 1778 to realise that most of the outline of the northwest coast of America that he was charting was insular was pointed out by his successors on the coast, but in deferential terms – not surprisingly, since most of them had sailed with Cook. An exception was Alexander Dalrymple, years earlier a rival for command of the *Endeavour* voyage, and a geographer whose view was bound to be influenced by the fact that Cook's first two voyages had destroyed his own hopes that a great southern continent existed. Now, after the third voyage, Dalrymple hoped to prove Cook wrong on the matter of a

Northwest Passage, and in a letter to a government official made his standpoint clear: 'I cannot admit of a Pope in Geography or Navigation'. Standing against him were the ranks of Cook's men who dominated the British voyages to the Pacific in the remaining years of the century. Bligh, Dixon, Portlock, Colnett, Riou, Hergest, Vancouver had all graduated in that most demanding of training schools, service with Cook. As William Wyndham, a senior government minister, exclaimed to Cook's old shipmate James Burney on hearing of Bligh's astonishing open-boat voyage after the mutiny on the *Bounty*: 'But what officers you are! You men of Captain Cook; you rise upon us in every trial.'

HAUNTED BY COOK

Respect for Cook was not confined to his seafaring countrymen. In France Louis XVI had a special edition of the voyages made for the edification of the Dauphin, while Marie Antoinette was reported to have selected *The Travels of Captain Cook* as one of the two books allowed her in the days before her execution. La Pérouse, whose voyage of 1785–88 was the *réplique française* or counter-stroke to Cook's voyages, was fulsome in his praise of the British navigator. His expedition was a follow-up to Cook's third voyage, and its instructions were a running commentary on what Cook had discovered and left undiscovered. As La Pérouse approached Hawai'i he entered in his journal:

> I shall always regard him as the first among navigators
> ... he is the real Christopher Columbus of this country,
> of the coast of Alaska and of almost all the islands of the
> South Sea.

A half-century later one of a long line of French naval explorers of the Pacific, Dumont d'Urville, wrote that he was 'haunted' by Cook: 'Nearly every night, I was tormented by dreams in which I saw myself on my third voyage around the world.'

Spanish attitudes towards Cook were more ambivalent. The Spanish government had not followed the French example of providing a safe conduct for Cook's ships on the third voyage; rather it had given instructions that they were to be intercepted and seized. This ambivalence can be seen in the journal of Alejandro Malaspina, who left Cadiz in 1789 on an ambitious 'scientific-political' expedition. In his proposal for the voyage, Malaspina stressed that the scientific part of the expedition would follow the models of the voyages of Cook and La Pérouse, as its officers and supernumeraries made hydrographic and astronomical observations and collected natural history specimens. In other ways, though, its political objectives of report and recommendation of reform in Spain's overseas empire marked it out from its British and French predecessors. As Malaspina explained, it would not be a traditional voyage of discovery at all, and, 'In no way should we wish to equate our voyage with those undertaken by Captain Cook.' Even so, with Cook's charts on board, comparisons were bound to be made. Off Cape Horn Malaspina set his own surveys in the context of Cook's: 'Once again we marvelled at the accuracy of Captain Cook's descriptions … guided as if by his own hand, we put aside any idea of discovery.' For all the humility of such declarations, rivalry with Britain still ran deep beneath the surface courtesies, and Malaspina's planned publication of the records of his voyage was intended to outshine even the splendid three-volume official account of

Cook's last voyage. In the first instance there would be seven volumes, an atlas of seventy charts, and a folio of seventy drawings, with additional volumes by the expedition's naturalists to follow. In the event only one, subsidiary, volume was published, for after his return to Spain Malaspina was tried for conspiracy against the Crown, and sentenced to life imprisonment.

In Russia, Cook's voyages were followed with special interest. His description of shipboard health measures on his second voyage was published at St Petersburg in 1778, and by the end of the century the accounts of all three voyages were available in Russian. As far as the third voyage was concerned Cook's incursion into northern waters was regarded with some suspicion. The reports from Kamchatka of strange ships sailing through Bering Strait in 1777/78 led to Ivan Kobelev being sent to investigate. He obtained a copy of the surveys left in Kamchatka by Captain Clerke, and produced an important map that showed his own explorations in the Bering Strait region as well as those of Cook and Clerke. The instructions of another planned Russian expedition at this time accused Cook of renaming 'places, lands and islands … previously discovered by Russians claiming them as his own discoveries', but this did little to affect the respect for Cook as a navigator. Junior crew members from Cook's last expedition, Joseph Billings (Able Seaman) and James Trevenen (Midshipman), were selected to command Russian survey expeditions to the North Pacific on the strength of the fact that they had sailed with Cook. Trevenen was diverted elsewhere, but Billings, accompanied by Kobelev, spent years engaged in detailed survey work.

Russia's Pacific navigators of the first half of the nineteenth century took Cook's voyages as their model. To Adam

Johann von Krusenstern, one of many Russian officers who had trained with the Royal Navy, and who commanded the first Russian circumnavigation in 1803–06, he was 'the great Cook' because of his superlative navigational skills. Similar phrases were used by Yuri Lisianskii, Commander of the consort vessel on the expedition, and by later circumnavigators such as Otto von Kotzebue and F.G. von Bellinghausen. In his introduction to Kotzebue's account of his round-the-world voyage of 1815–18 Krusenstern brought hero-worship to new heights of adulation when he wrote 'that which was impossible to Cook would hardly be possible for another'. In similar vein Adelbert von Chamisso, the naturalist on Kotzebue's expedition, recollected:

> In my childhood Cook had lifted the curtain that still concealed an enticing world of marvels, and I could not imagine that extraordinary man in any other fashion than clothed in light.

The Russian navigators in the Pacific not only copied many of Cook's practices – especially in matters of health and diet – but they stopped at places visited by Cook, his accounts and charts in hand, and insisted on using the names he had given to locations many years before. At Kealakekua Bay in 1804 Lisianskii 'landed at the very rock on which this truly great man lost his life', and found flattened musket balls in the trees lining the beach. He was followed by Golovnin, who in 1818 stood on the same rock, saw the gaps made by the cannon balls fired from Cook's ships, and heard how King Kamehameha ('an ordinary chief' in 1779) had told 'the story with all the details, how it all happened, where Cook stood, how he fell on his face in the water, and so forth'.

Elsewhere there were happier associations. So at Matavai Bay in Tahiti Kotzebue set up his observatory on Cape Venus at 'precisely the same spot where Cook's Observatory had formerly been erected'. Simon Werrett has argued that for these naval officers (many of them forming a distinct group of highly educated Baltic Germans within Russian society) Cook was another Napoleon

and the voyage of exploration a kind of battlefield, another fluid space of adventure where the officer might overcome great odds to achieve his place in history next to the 'immortal Cook'.

A PLACE BECOME TOO REMARKABLY FAMOUS

Of all the places in the Pacific associated with Cook, the dramatic amphitheatre of Kealakekua Bay with its lava foreshore and dark, beetling cliffs inevitably attracted most sightseers, many in the guise of pilgrims or mourners. James King anticipated this future interest when he wrote only a few days after Cook's death that Kealakekua Bay was already 'a place become too remarkably famous'. Six years passed after the forlorn departure of the *Resolution* and *Discovery* in February 1779 before another European vessel visited Hawai'i. When Nathaniel Portlock, bound for the northwest coast of America in the trader *King George*, reached Kealakekua Bay in May 1786, he became the first in a long line of visitors from the sea for whom the spot would always be associated with the death of Cook. Some of the arrivals were Cook's men – Portlock himself who had been Master's Mate on the *Discovery* on Cook's last voyage, and Colnett, Dixon and Vancouver. Others had never sailed with Cook, and many were not British at all, but all treated Kealakekua Bay as a place with a special meaning.

Portlock sighted Hawai'i on 24 May 1786 and headed for Kealakekua Bay since that was the island's only known anchorage. There was tension between the crew and those islanders who came out to the ship in their canoes, 'and seemed by their behaviour to think that we were come to revenge the death of captain Cook'. With the islanders beginning to behave in 'a very daring and insolent manner', Portlock decided not to land in the bay, but fired warning shots at the canoes to make them keep their distance, and stood three leagues offshore to trade. Unknown to Portlock, the discovery expedition of La Pérouse was also in the islands in 1786, but the French commander avoided Hawai'i altogether because of his 'regret at the loss of so great a man'. Instead he headed for Maui where he anchored in the bay now named after him. Even here La Pérouse admitted that he was prejudiced against the inhabitants because of the events seven years earlier at Kealakekua Bay, and when he went ashore was guarded by soldiers with fixed bayonets. However, during his brief visit he found the islanders 'gentle and considerate', and when reflecting on what he had read of Cook's death wondered 'whether some imprudent action of his part did not, in some way, compel the inhabitants of *Owhyee* to have recourse to a justified defence'.

In August 1787 John Meares, a former naval lieutenant trading to the northwest coast of America in the *Nootka*, spent a month in Hawai'i, and found a very different atmosphere from that which Portlock had recorded. Rather, the islanders' welcome was reminiscent of that given to Cook in January 1779.

The numbers of them which surrounded the ship with a view to obtain permission to go to *Britannee*, to the friends of their beloved Cook, are incredible ... Presents were poured in on us from the chiefs, who were prevented by the multitude from approaching the vessel, and the clamorous cry of *Britannee, Britannee*, was for a long time heard from every part, without ceasing.

On board the *Nootka* as it left the islands for China was 'Tianna' or Kaiana, a chief of Kauai. While the vessel was at Whampoa, Kaiana's portrait was painted by a Chinese artist, and this prompted Meares into a digression about Cook's visit to Hawai'i.

When this painting was presented to him [Kaiana], he received it with a degree of solemnity that struck all who beheld it; and then, in a state of agitation in which he had never been seen by us, he mentioned the catastrophe which deprived the world of Captain Cook. He now, for the first time, informed us that a fierce war had been waged throughout the Islands, on account of a painting which he called a portrait of that great man, and which had been left with one of their most potent chiefs. The painting, he added, was held sacred amongst them as the only retribution they could make for their unfortunate destruction of the original.

Meares was never reluctant to tell a good story, and there is no other evidence of the existence of a painting of Cook done in Hawai'i.

On his visit to Kealakekua Bay in December 1788 another British trader, William Douglas, found that significant changes had occurred in the ten years since Cook's visit. Kalani'opu'u was dead; and his successor, soon to be known as Kamehameha I after his conquest of all the Hawaiian Islands except Kauai, claimed that Kalani'opu'u had been poisoned for his part in Cook's death. Douglas had no way of knowing whether or not this was true, but he was reassured to welcome on board the *Iphigenia* 'the faithful Eappo [Yappo], who may be remembered as having brought the bones of the illustrious navigator to Captain Clerke'.

Everywhere in the Hawaiian Islands there were reminders of Cook. In February 1788 James Colnett, who had sailed as a midshipman on Cook's second voyage, and was now captain of the trader *King George*, reached Waimea Bay on the island of Kauai. There memories of the death of Cook hung heavily over the relations between the islanders and crew as the journals of Colnett and his mate Andrew Taylor show. Taylor recorded that on 17 February Typowooah, 'an inferior Chief' from Hawai'i, brought on board a ruffled shirt supposedly worn by Cook or 'ye Oronno Nuez' (the Great Lono) when he was killed. The chief maintained that he had been near Cook when he fell. The shirt, which was stained with blood, had several holes and slits in it, but Taylor noticed that the holes and blood marks did not correspond, and was doubtful whether the garment was worn by Cook on the day of his death. Rather, he thought that it might have been given away by Cook as a gift, and then used to wrap some of his remains. Even so, Colnett described how

> our Seamen were anxious to examine the Shirt, while each listened to the direful tale and countenance of each was a true index of the feelings of their susceptible Hearts ...

every sailor present, however callous on any other occasion was sensibly affected.

Colnett added that the chief had long been detested by all
the Crew

after informing us he was the man Captain Cook fired
the Small Shot at, & shewed us several marks which he
said he left, also told us he gave him the Blow which
occasion'd his Death.

Writing much later, John Nicol, cooper on the *King George*,
added details that hardly fit with Colnett's account of the
crew's attitude:

We had the chief on board who killed Captain Cook for
more than three weeks. He was in bad health, and had a
smelling-bottle with a few drops in it which he used to
smell at. We filled it for him.

The list of those supposed to have killed Cook grew with
almost every enquiry. James Trevenen was told that the man
who first stabbed Cook was 'an old Chief, whom Captn
Cook had himself kicked out of the Ship that day before with
many expressions of anger for having committed a theft',
and that he was shot on the spot by a marine. David Samwell
had another candidate, a leading chief called Noo-ah (Nu'a),
who was a relative and 'constant companion' of the King. In
his later published account he described him as

tall and stout, with a fierce look and demeanour, and one
who united in his figure the two qualities of strength and

agility, to a greater degree, than ever I remembered to have seen before in any other man.

This was written in 1786 and one wonders whether it was a genuine recollection by Samwell (who was not present at the scene of Cook's death) or a description of the muscular figure about to stab Cook in Webber's famous painting. Samwell added that the man who first struck Cook with a club was another chief, Ka-rima-no-co-a-ha, and in an aside that contradicted Trevenen's assertion that Nu'a had been shot dead, maintained that a priest had told him that both assailants were still 'held in great esteem on account of that action'.

The first Royal Navy ships to visit Hawai'i after Cook were commanded by George Vancouver, who had been on Cook's second and third voyages, and regarded himself as the great explorer's successor. In March 1792 Vancouver's ships, the *Discovery* and the *Chatham*, were off Kealakekua Bay, but did not land there. The *Chatham*'s clerk, Edward Bell, wrote, '... we stood pretty near the Shore – and were pointed out the Spot where that horrid melancholy Massacre was committed.' The following February the expedition visited Kealakekua Bay, where they were greeted by King Kamehameha I. Vancouver recorded how 'his Owhyhean majesty' came out to the ships at the head of a flotilla of canoes,

> dressed in a printed linen gown that Captain Cook had given to [Kalani'opu'u], and the most elegant feathered cloak I had yet seen ... On his head he wore a very handsome helmet, and made altogether a very magnificent appearance.

The next month Vancouver visited the spot where Cook had been killed:

> This melancholy, and ever to be deplored event, the natives are at much pains to represent, to reproduce reasons for its taking place, and to shew that it fulfilled the prophecies of the priests, who had foretold this sad catastrophe.

Further comment, Vancouver wrote, he would defer 'to future consideration'; but if he made such comment it never found its way into his journal.

Among the other officers and crew, Bell and Peter Puget, First Lieutenant of the *Discovery* and then Commander of the *Chatham*, seem to have been most assiduous in tracing local recollections of Cook. In March 1793 Puget, Bell and some others visited the 'rock' in Kealakekua Bay where Cook had been killed. Bell noted of the event that 'every child able to prattle can give you an account of it' – perhaps not the best recommendation of the reliability of the information – and produced another, unnamed individual as Cook's killer:

> In one of the Canoes that here came off to us, a man was pointed out to us, as being the principal hand in the murder of Captain Cook, and as such, it is natural to be supposed, he was not a little stared at, which he observed, and stole away, and we saw nothing more of him. He was a tall, stout man, of a fierce countenance.

Puget also saw a man who was supposed to have killed Cook, but identified him as Palea, who had featured prominently in the accounts of Cook's stay at Kealakekua Bay, and who had been knocked unconscious in the scuffle with a boat's crew the evening before Cook's death. Rather bizarrely, Puget reported, 'some of the Gentlemen requested a lock of his hair'. Joshua Dimsdell, a former quartermaster who was living in Hawai'i at the time of Vancouver's visit, put forward yet another name, that of Pihere, who was 'a strong Raw Boned man above the Common Size'. Although he admitted his part in the deed, he 'added with Tears that he hoped the Orono would forgive him – as he had built several Morai's to his Memory, and sacrificed a number of Hogs at each of them'. By now, one is tempted to think that almost any Hawaiian of above-average height living near Kealakekua Bay might be identified as the man who had killed Captain Cook.

Vancouver, who after all had not been far distant at the time of Cook's death, seems to have agreed that Palea was the guilty person. In 1794 he took no action against him, and let him come on board the ship. Inter-island warfare had reduced him to 'a very low and abject condition', and Vancouver wrote that he was prepared to forget 'all former injuries and offences'. As the expedition sailed from Kealakekua Bay Vancouver made one last reference to the significance of the spot. Despite its melancholy memories, 'to us it had proved an asylum, where the hospitable reception, and friendly treatment were such as could not have been surpassed by the most enlightened nation of the earth.'

Later visitors added further, mostly contradictory, details about Cook's death. William Mariner, a ship's clerk living in Tonga from 1806 to 1810 after his vessel had been seized by islanders, picked up a story from Hawaiians living in Tonga that Cook had been killed by a carpenter who failed to realise that he was 'the extraordinary being of whom he had heard so much, for he lived a considerable distance up the country'. An American seaman, George Little, struck an original if mystifying note when he claimed to have visited in February 1809 Cook's grave, which from his description bore no resemblance to the area around the stone *heiau* at Kealakekua Bay where Cook's remains were supposedly buried. It was, Little wrote,

> a beautiful, sequestered spot, of a circular form, surrounded with banana and cocoa-nut trees, the grave occupying the centre of the circle. The natives, on approaching this place, seemed to be awed into a profound reverence ... once in every year, all the natives assembled here to perform a religious rote in memory of his lamentable death.

The nearest to an official visit to Hawai'i came with the arrival in 1825 of *HMS Blonde*, commanded by Captain (Lord) Byron, cousin of the poet. The vessel carried the bodies of Kamehameha II and his queen, Kamalulu, who had both become ill and died on an official visit to London. On board was an artist, Robert Dampier, who recorded that the ship made a detour to Kealakekua Bay 'to gratify our curiosity in the contemplation of the scene of Cook's calamitous death'. There a local chief, Nahi, who lived within a few yards of the spot where Cook was killed, told Dampier that as a boy he had witnessed Cook's death. The man who struck him down was a commoner from another part of the island, 'ignorant of Cook's attributed Divinity'. Those involved in the fracas

> regretted exceedingly what they had done. They even

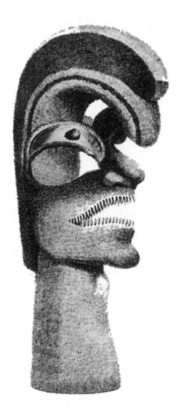

16. Hawaiian idol by John Webber, 1784. Described by James King as 'made of basket work, variously covered with red, black, white, and Yellow feathers, the Eyes represent'd by a bit of Pearl Oyster Shell with a black button, & the teeth were those of dogs, the mouths of all were strangely distorted, as well as other features.'

now look upon this event as a sort of national stigma upon their character & generally endeavour to evade all conversation relating to it.

Before he left, Byron erected a memorial to Cook in the form of an inscribed copper plate, let into a cross ten feet high, which was set up above the beach. The inscription was a minimal affair:

> Sacred to the Memory of Capt. Cook, R.N. (who discover'd these islands in the year of our Lord 1778), this humble monument is erected by his countrymen in the year of our Lord 1825.

As the harbour of Honolulu on Oahu increased in importance, so fewer vessels called at Kealakekua Bay, 'an insecure & unpleasant anchorage' according to Dampier; but those who did invariably made for the spot where Cook had been killed. In 1839 Captain John Shepherd of the *Sparrowhawk* erected a commemorative plaque, and carried away pieces of rock while 'endeavouring to call to mind the scenes of which this most interesting spot had once been the theatre'. Among later visitors was Lady Jane Franklin, widow of the Arctic explorer, whose companion described not only Byron's memorial as it appeared in 1861 but also the stump of a palm tree covered with copper sheathing on which was scratched the names of Royal Navy ships that had visited a place 'so deeply interesting to Englishmen'.

When Mark Twain visited the bay five years later to write an article for a Californian newspaper the monument set up by Byron was in poor shape,

> a thing like a guideboard ... on a tall pole, and formerly there was an inscription upon it describing the memorable occurrence that had there taken place but the sun and wind have long ago so defaced it as to render it illegible.

However, as he wandered around the beach Twain came

across the uprooted stump of a palm tree stored in a tumbledown building. This was, supposedly, the remains of the tree cut in half by a cannon ball from the *Resolution* after Cook was killed. When Twain saw it, the inscriptions on the copper sheets were barely legible. The pathetic stump was, he wrote with heavy irony, 'the touching tribute [and] symbol of a nation's gratitude'. He left it to his fictional companion, Brown, to point the contrast between 'this old rotten chunk' of wood and the huge and expensive monument recently built in London to honour Prince Albert. Twain's words are a reminder that suggestions that Cook should be commemorated by a memorial in Westminster Abbey had come to nothing (although two hundred years after his death a Navigators Memorial was unveiled in the south cloister of the Abbey, dedicated to three circumnavigators – Francis Drake, Francis Chichester, and Cook).

CHIEF OF THE AIR, EARTH, WATER

The extraordinary scenes that greeted Cook's arrival in Hawai'i in 1779 were not typical of his reception elsewhere in the Pacific. Cook's treatment varied according to time, place and circumstance. Throughout Polynesia a high chief's status stemmed from his ancestors, who in ages past had come from distant lands. When Cook's ships arrived at places unvisited by Europeans, the great vessels with their tree-like masts were often assumed to be the marvellous floating islands that prophecy said would one day come from the far-off homeland. Their commanders were *atua* or *akua*, supernatural beings, and as such were greeted by the priests with ritual offerings, while the attendant crews were *tupua* or goblins. Elsewhere in the Pacific there might be a different identification of the strange visitors, so in the New Hebrides (Vanuatu) and New Caledonia Cook and his crew were taken to be ghosts. On the east coast of Australia the Aboriginal peoples seemed, unusually, to show not the slightest interest in the arrival of the strange ship, and Cook found this both worrying and inexplicable. Only for a few days at Endeavour River was there cautious contact between the ship's crew and the local inhabitants, and this soon ceased after a quarrel over the 'theft' of a turtle. Even more distant from Polynesia, at Nootka Sound on Vancouver Island, the initial reaction of the Nuu-chah-nulth people to Cook's arrival was a mixture of curiosity and apprehension as they struggled to come to terms with the appearance of his ships, identified by different watchers as great salmon alive with people, huge seagulls, or sea serpents controlled by the moon. Once the alien beings were recognised as men, a relationship based on trade quickly developed.

On all three of Cook's voyages there was no doubt who was the 'chief' of the newcomers. On the *Endeavour* voyage, despite the exuberance of Banks, most Polynesians saw that Cook was clearly the leader of the strangers. Only the shipboard presence of the Raiatean priest-navigator Tupa'ia (offered a passage to England by Banks) presented a challenge to Cook's authority, and that seems to have been a perception confined to New Zealand Maori. Otherwise, as his ship anchored in some island bay Cook was always first to land, advancing with gestures of friendship towards the group of wary warriors lining the shore. Midshipman John Elliott described how Cook

would land alone unarm'd, or lay aside his Arms, and sit down, when they threaten'd with theirs, throwing them

Beads, Knives, and other little presents, then by degrees advancing nearer, till by Patience, and forbearance, he gain'd their friendship.

On the second voyage it would have been obvious to all that the deferential Furneaux in the *Adventure* was subordinate to Cook, and in any case his ship lost company with the *Resolution* during the voyage and returned home early. On the third voyage Cook's fellow captain, the once zestful Charles Clerke, was so ill that he rarely ventured on shore. If the later report of the missionary John Williams is correct, so dominant was Cook's personality that in Tahiti newcomers were all called 'Cookees' – as explained by a Tahitian woman, who made it clear to Rarotongans that '*they* were not the only people in the world, that there were others entirely white, whom they called Cookees, that Captain Cook had been to her island'.

Unsurprisingly then, it was Cook who in Tahiti, Hawai'i and other islands entered into ceremonial friendships with the high chiefs, exchanging names and gifts. On the first voyage Cook became the *taio* – the friend, equal, ally – of Tutaha in Tahiti. At Huahine on the second voyage Cook renewed his acquaintanceship with the aged chief, Ori, who 'fell upon my neck and embraced me'. Cook added,

this was by no means ceremonious, the tears which trinckled [sic] plentifully down his Cheeks sufficiently spoke the feelings of his heart ... [he] receiv'd me more like a son he had not seen these four years than a friend.

A few days later there were more tears from the chief as Anders Sparrman, the young Swedish naturalist, was assaulted while on shore and stripped of his clothes. Ori insisted on putting himself in Cook's power by going on board the *Resolution* until the most valuable of the stolen possessions were restored. The episode showed, Cook wrote, that 'friendship is sacred with these people', before admitting that 'we however may never meet with another chief who will act in the same manner'.

At Tahiti in April 1774 as soon as Cook anchored at Matavai Bay the *Resolution* was overrun with 'old friends'. It was the astronomer William Wales, more sceptical – at least in his journal – than Cook, who while agreeing that 'they were extreamly glad to see us', added a rider, 'from what Motive I will not pretend to say'. On his side, Cook wrote of the arrival at the bay of the great chief Tu:

> Knowing how much it was to my intrest to make this man my friend, I met him at the Tents and conducted him and his friends on board in my boat where they stayed dinner, after which they were dismissed with Suitable presents and highly pleased with the reception they met with.

At one level Cook's motives in establishing or confirming friendships with island chiefs were strictly practical: he needed a harbour where he could obtain provisions, carry out astronomical observations, and refresh his crew – in safety. The protection of the chiefs could not always guarantee this, but without their goodwill the many incidents of petty thieving might have turned into something altogether more serious and threatening. At a different level Cook's curiosity about the peoples of the Pacific grew by the month, and his attempts at understanding their customs would have been impossible without the goodwill of the chiefs. Unfortunately, an enthusiastic welcome could be as distracting to serious investigation as open hostility. On the third voyage the surgeon William Anderson remarked of the clamorous reception at Atiu in the Cook Islands:

> We regretted much that their behaviour prevented us from making any observations on the country, for we were seldom a hundred yards from the place where we were introduc'd to the chiefs on landing.

The arrival of the ships halted the normal processes of living, for as Cook reflected gloomily in Tonga, 'It was always holyday.'

Polynesian attempts at establishing friendly relations with the visitors had several dimensions. Fear was undoubtedly one. From the moment the cannon of Wallis's *Dolphin* wrought carnage among the islanders on the first visit by a European vessel to Tahiti in 1767, the threat of superior force was an element in the relationship. Once chiefs were confident that guns would not be turned on them they were often eager to enlist the firepower of their formidable visitors against local enemies. In August 1777 at Tahiti on the third voyage, Tu's council of chiefs tried to enlist Cook's support in the war against the neighbouring island of Eimeo (Moorea), and with no interpreter to hand Cook was obliged to explain as best he could that 'as I was not thoroughly acquainted with the dispute and the people of Eimeo having never offended me I could take no part in it'. In material terms the ships were floating treasure-houses to the islanders. Iron was prized above all, and if it could not be obtained by exchange, then it was stolen. The theft of the *Discovery*'s

114 THE DEATH OF CAPTAIN COOK

cutter at Kealakekua Bay a few hours before Cook's death was undoubtedly prompted by the amount of iron contained in its fittings. Nails were prime items of barter, to the extent that a ship's structure might be weakened by their removal from the hull by crew members desperate for sex or intent on acquiring 'curiosities'. Apart from iron, other desirable trade goods were more difficult to predict, and values fluctuated according to laws of supply and demand. Most profitable from the crew's point of view were the red feathers obtained by the bagful in Tonga on the second and third voyages and which were found to be madly in demand for ritual purposes in Tahiti. For a while, a few feathers were enough to procure a fifty-pound hog. A Borabora chief, Tai, an old acquaintance of Mai's, ignored the wanderer on his return to the Society Islands in 1777, until he realised that Mai had a stock of red feathers. Immediately, he begged that they might become *taios* and exchange names, and presented Mai with a hog. Cynics might see in this episode a more general explanation for the establishment of *taio* relationships between island chiefs and Cook, but there was more to their eagerness than this. As Nicholas Thomas has suggested, 'What they were trying to collect, control and assimilate was rather his name, his image and an idea of his prestige.'

How far Cook's personality played a part in the Poly-nesian reaction to the arrival of his ships is difficult to assess. On the third voyage David Samwell thought that Cook's fairness in dealing with disputes between his crew and the islanders 'rendered him highly respected & esteemed by all the Indians', while Rickman went a stage further with his comment that by Cook's

impartial distribution of equal justice, the Indians

themselves conceived so high an idea of his wisdom, and his power too, that they paid him the honours as they did their Et-hua-a, or good spirit.

But it was on this voyage that Cook ordered such severe punishments on individuals and communities that his behaviour has been likened to that of some of the Polynesian chiefs whose capricious actions the visitors deplored. Samwell wrote that Cook was 'dreaded' as well as 'esteemed', and that his name 'will be handed down to Posterity as the greatest Chief & a man of the greatest Power that ever visited their Island'. After the destruction of the islanders' canoes on Moorea in October 1777, King wrote that 'in future they may fear, but never love us'. The crew's half-joking use of 'Tute', the Polynesian version of 'Cook', when referring to their captain had implications about his behaviour that were not altogether flattering.

Cook has been justly praised for his efforts to prevent the spread of venereal disease, and by his self-discipline in personally keeping aloof from all forms of sexual contact. However, it is not clear how Polynesian women regarded this commanding figure, this prized trophy who steadfastly resisted all their blandishments. At Nomuka on the second voyage, a Tongan couple tried unsuccessfully to persuade Cook to go off with a lively young 'Miss', and his refusal brought a stream of abuse from the older woman:

> I understood very little of what she said, but her actions were expressive enough and shew'd that her words were to this effect, Sneering in my face and saying, what sort of man are you thus to refuse the embraces of so fine a young Woman.

One of Cook's midshipmen noted of 'our fair friends', 'I have often seen them jeer and laugh at him, calling him Old, and good for nothing.' That this was not a universal attitude was shown by the treatment Cook experienced on his last visit to Tahiti in September 1777 when a formidable party consisting of Tu's wife, three sisters, and eight other women came on board to rid him of rheumatic pain that affected his side from the hip downwards. For two days they gave Cook a series of massages so vigorous that 'they made my bones crack and a perfect Mummy of my flesh', but by the end they had cured Tu's *taio*.

During his years of Pacific voyaging Cook felt that he had become familiar with many diverse responses from the local populations, but Hawai'i was different from anything that he had experienced before. At Kealakekua Bay the puzzled crews watched deference to their commander turn into a more elaborate and unexpected type of ceremonial greeting. At Kauai a year earlier Cook realised that the islanders had not seen Europeans before:

> I never saw Indians so much astonished at the entering a ship before, their eyes were continually flying from object to object, the wildness of their looks and actions fully express'd their surprise and astonishment at the several new objects before them and evinced that they had never been on board of a ship before.

Later Hawaiian accounts describe the excitement and uncertainty among the inhabitants of Kauai as the ships first came into view. At one moment they compared their appearance to giant stingrays, at another to trees floating in the water. One possibility, perhaps recollected with the advantage of hindsight, was they were the canoes of Lono, an ancestral king or high chief who had fled to Tahiti generations before, but who promised to return. Unaware of these comparisons, the next morning, 21 January 1778, Cook went ashore for the first time in the Hawaiian archipelago. Unlike the landing at Kealakekua Bay a year later, we can follow events on Kauai in Cook's own words:

> As soon as the Ships was anchored I went a shore with three boats, to look at the water and try the desposition of the inhabitants, several hundreds of whom were assembled on a sandy beach before the village. The very instant I leaped ashore, they all fell flat on their faces, and remained in that humble posture till I made signs to them to rise. They then brought a great many small pigs and gave us without regarding whether they got any thing in return ...

Prostration was the customary sign of respect paid to high chiefs or kings in the Hawaiian Islands, but it had not been experienced by Cook before. The next day he went inland a little way and inspected a *heiau* or temple, which he remarked was similar to a Tahitian *marae*. Part of it was covered with white *tapa* cloth,

> which seemed to be consecrated to Religious and ceremonious purposes, as a good deal of it was about this Morai and I had some of it forced upon me on my first landing.

There is a slightly uneasy recognition here by Cook that, with or without his consent, he had been greeted with something more than the usual tribute paid to a high chief. On 1 February he landed at the neighbouring island of Nihau, where he presented two pigs to a group of islanders on the beach,

> on which the Chief began to mutter something like a prayer and the two men with the pigs continued to walk round me all the time, not less than ten or a dozen times before the other had finished. This ceremony being ended, we proceeded and presently met people coming from all parts, who, on the men with me calling to them laid down till I was out of sight.

Cook's reception at Kealakekua Bay in January 1779 introduced an altogether new dimension. The tumultuous scenes as the ships anchored, the mass prostrations on the beach, Cook's elevation at the great stone *heiau* at Hikiau, the escort of priests, and the continual chants of 'Lono' gave the occasion all the appearance of a religious festival. David Samwell described how:

> To day a Ceremony was performed by the Priests in which he was invested by them with the Title and Dignity of Orono, which is the highest Rank among these Indians and is a Character that is looked upon by them as partaking something of divinity.

Lieutenant King noted that 'Erono' was the name by which Cook was 'distinguish'd by the Natives'. The question was: who or what was Orono, Erono or Lono? Confusingly, if Ledyard's recollection is accurate, when Kalani'opu'u appeared he was also greeted with cries of 'Lono Lahi' (Great Lono), and according to Samwell's understanding 'the Title of

Orono which is esteemed sacred among them' belonged only to the King and his family. When Kalani'opu'u met Cook on 26 January they exchanged names as well as gifts; were they therefore both Lono, and if so what were the implications of the joint dignity? No member of the expedition had an answer to these questions. When at a later date James King described the events of these days in the authorised account he clearly felt that he could not leave the matter totally unexplained, and he added a footnote in which he tried to represent shipboard views on Lono.

> Captain Cook generally went by this name among the natives of Owhyhee; but we could never hear its precise meaning. Sometimes they applied it to an invisible being, who, they said, lived in the heavens. We also found that it was a title belonging to a personage of great rank and power in the island, who resembles pretty much the Dalai Lama of the Tartars, and the ecclesiastical emperor of Japan.

With its suggestion of the mingling of the religious and the secular this was as near to the complicated reality of the Hawaiian situation as any outsider got for many years. Even today, scholars differ in emphasis on the Lono issue, and in particular – to put it at its simplest – whether Cook was being given the status of a high chief or that of a god (*akua*). In 1779 Cook's men had no idea that there was a sacred yearly cycle in Hawai'i in which Ku the god of war dominated one season before giving way to Lono, god of peace and fertility, in the other; and that Cook had arrived in Lono's time bearing what Hawaiians recognised as his insignia. On one side Cook was concerned with refitting and replenishing his ships, and grateful for the help offered by the islanders. On the other, the Hawaiians were welcoming the long-awaited return of Lono, a mythical figure from the past. On each side there was genuine ignorance about the assumptions of the other.

As baffling to the crews as any of the happenings during the first weeks of their stay was what the crews saw as the wildly inconsistent behaviour of the Hawaiians after Cook's death. Some wept and expressed sorrow, pledging to recover his body; others taunted the crews, waving Cook's hat in defiance, baring their buttocks, hurling stones. Still more puzzling was the repeated questioning as to when Lono would return. Kalani'opu'u never appeared in person, but on 19 February he sent one of his sons on board the *Resolution* with some of Cook's remains. The next day the son returned in the company of Hiapo, who said he was acting on Kalani'opu'u's behalf. In Lieutenant King's words the two men 'were very inquisitive if we meant to return & what we should then do, & indeed were anxious to know whether we always would be friends'. King has more to say about Kalani'opu'u in the authorised account than he recorded in his daily journal. He

> retired to a cave in the steep part of the mountain, that hangs over the bay, which was accessible only by the help of ropes, and where he remained for many days, having had his victuals let down to him by ropes.

The usual interpretation is that the King was in mourning for Cook, although it may well be that his seclusion was a reaction to the deaths of so many Hawaiians, including five chiefs.

Cook's remains were treated in the same way as those of a royal sacrificial victim or high-status adversary in which the corpse was dismembered, flesh burned and thrown away, and the bones distributed among the chiefs. The *tabu* man and his companion who came on board the *Resolution* on the night of the 15th with their ghastly parcel of flesh explained to King that this was all they could get of Cook's body, and that most of the rest was in the possession of Kalani'opu'u and the other chiefs. When George Vancouver's expedition visited Hawai'i in 1793 Lieutenant Puget was told that Cook's remains were buried, along with those of Kalani'opu'u, at the stone *heiau* at Hikiau, and that, 'The Memory of Capt. Cook appears on all occasions to be treated with the Greatest Veneration by all Ranks of People.' A similar story appears in the recollections of Joshua Dimsdell, the former quarter-master who lived in Hawaii from 1792 onwards:

> There are a Variety of Morais built to his Memory in several parts of the Island & the Natives sacrifice to him in Common with their other Dieties. It is their firm Hope and Belief that he will come again & forgive them. He is never mentioned but with the utmost reverence.

The return of Cook/Lono was a recurrent theme. When James Colnett visited Hawai'i in 1791 islanders attributed recent wars, outbreaks of disease and volcanic eruptions to a revengeful Cook, and asked Colnett 'how long he would be angry with them'. For his part, Dimsdell was the only non-Hawaiian to claim that he had seen Cook's bones. They were in the possession of Kamehameha I, and he had been allowed to see them 'as a great favour'. One might be inclined to distrust this story were it not for the oddly convincing detail that the bones 'were perhaps ⅔ of the Human frame or not quite so much'. The disposal of Cook's bones marked the beginning rather than the end of the story of the explorer's reputation on Hawai'i, and it would not be long before other visitors to Kealakekua Bay heard much more about his life, death, and afterlife.

Away from Hawai'i there was a less publicised side to Cook's visits. In some islands – the Marquesas, the Easter Islands, the Cook Islands, Tonga – there was no veneration and sometimes very little respect. At some Cook did not land, so the question of his status did not arise, but even on islands familiar to him there might be danger. At Raiatea in November 1777 he and Clerke narrowly escaped a plan to seize them in revenge for their having taken hostage Poeatua, the daughter of the chief. In a rare journal entry about his personal habits, Cook explained that 'it was my custom to go and bathe in the fresh Water every evening, and very often alone and without arms'. Cook's suspicions were aroused by the chief's insistent questioning about when he was going to bathe, and then a young woman from another island warned a sailor on the *Discovery* about the plot. Earlier in the voyage Cook had unwittingly exchanged names with a minor chief rather than with the paramount chief at Lifuka in the Tongan archipelago, and had then upset his hosts by his intrusive behaviour at the sacred *inasi* ceremony at Tongatapu. Despite the cries of *tabu* and demands that he should leave the scene Cook insisted on watching proceedings, to the evident disquiet of his hosts (and the disapproval of Lieutenant Williamson). Many years later the missionary John Thomas heard about Cook's violation of the sacred ceremony, and remarked that since the priests were 'full of fear for their gods, the wonder is that the Captain escaped

being struck, or killed'. Elsewhere in the Tongan archipelago there seems to have been another plot to kill Cook and
seize his ships. The story comes from William Mariner, and
although there is no corroborating evidence for his information, which he claimed came from the son of the chief most
involved in the plot, there seems no reason why he should
have invented it. Cook and his officers were to be invited
to a night dance at which they would be massacred under
cover of darkness and the ships seized. Fortunately, a dis-
agreement among the chiefs as to the timing of the operation
led to the abandonment of the scheme, and Cook, unaware
of his narrow escape, named (misnamed, Mariner said) the
archipelago the Friendly Islands.

In New Zealand there is an account by Horeta Te Taniwha
of the arrival of the *Endeavour* at Whitianga on the North
Island in November 1769. Te Taniwha was a small boy at the
time, but listened as the old men said that the ship 'was an
atua, a god, and the people on board were tupua, strange
people or goblins', who clearly had eyes in the back of their
heads since they rowed their boats with their backs to the
bows. As canoes came out to trade with the newcomers one
warrior offered Lieutenant Gore a dogskin cloak in exchange
for a piece of cloth. Having secured the cloth he refused to
honour the rest of the transaction. Te Taniwha recounted
what happened next:

> They paddled away. The goblin went down into the hold
> of the ship, but soon came up with a walking-stick in his
> hand, and pointed with it at the canoe that was paddling
> away. Thunder pealed and lightning flashed, but those
> in the canoe paddled on. When they landed eight rose
> to leave the canoe, but the thief sat still with his dogskin

mat and the garment of the goblin under his feet. His companions called to him, but he did not answer. One of them went and shook him, and the thief fell back into the hold of the canoe, and blood was seen on his clothing and a hole in his back.

Te Taniwha went on to say much about the deadly 'walking-sticks', and the even more terrifying great guns fired from the ship, but the best-known part of his account concerns Cook:

> There was one supreme man in that ship. We knew that he was the lord of the whole by his perfect gentlemanly and noble demeanour. He seldom spoke, but some of the goblins spoke much ... He was a very good man, and came to us – the children – and patted our cheeks, and gently touched our heads.

In a longer version of the account, Cook gave Te Taniwha a nail, which he used as a point to his spear and which he carried with him wherever he went, until one day, 'I was in a canoe and she capsized in the sea, and my god [the nail] was lost to me.'

There are problems about such recollections. This one was noted down by an Englishman (hence the use of English terms) in the 1850s when Te Taniwha was in his 'eighties and would have heard much about the famous Captain Cook he had seen as a child'. There are other interpretations of the strange vessel and its occupants, though all hint at some supernatural status for the newcomers. A few weeks before the Whitianga landing the *Endeavour* had anchored for the first time in New Zealand waters, at Poverty Bay (Turanganui). There, according to local traditions, again recorded long after the event, it was assumed by some to be a floating island, by others to be a great bird, perhaps the same that had carried their ancestors from their mythical homeland of Hawaiki.

On Cook's second voyage there were similar reactions when Maori saw the newcomers for the first time. George Forster describes how in Dusky Sound in South Island in April 1773 Cook encountered a man and two women. When Cook approached the little group the man 'trembled very visibly' and showed 'strong marks of fear'. By the time of Cook's third voyage, there were noticeable changes in attitude on both sides. The killing of the *Adventure*'s boat crew at Grass Cove in 1773, coming hard on the heels of the deaths of the French explorer Marion du Fresne and some of his crew at the Bay of Islands the year before, had widespread repercussions. In both incidents there was a build-up of tension following the taking of local resources without consent and the violation of *tabu* by the newcomers, set against increasing challenges and widespread 'pilfering' by the local inhabitants. Maori ceased to treat the strangers as supernatural beings, for if any confirmation was needed that the newcomers were not *atua* or gods, the ease with which they were killed seemed ample proof. But the impact of Grass Cove went further than this. Both Maori and his own crew were puzzled by Cook's decision when he revisited Dusky Sound on his third voyage not to use his superior weaponry to punish the perpetrators. He even allowed Kahura, leader of the attackers in 1773, on the *Resolution*, where Webber drew his portrait, and took on board two young Maori as crew members. While the crew gave vent to their anger by putting on trial and executing a 'cannibal dog', puzzled Maori, in Burney's words,

held us in great contempt, and I believe chiefly on account
of our not revenging the affair of Grass Cove, so contrary
to the principles by which they would have been actu-
ated in the like case.

The New Zealand anthropologist and historian, Anne
Salmond, who has investigated the affair in detail, shows
that soon after the violent encounters of 1772 and 1773 the
present-day terms 'Maori' and 'Pakeha' emerged to distinguish between the two peoples, between those who are ordinary, local and familiar, and those who although human are
extraordinary and unfamiliar.

Whatever status Cook was given in later recollections,
there is no doubt that in certain places and at certain times
during the *Endeavour*'s circuit of New Zealand, Tupa'ia, the
remarkable Raiatean priest-navigator, attracted more attention than Cook. The ship was widely assumed to be his, which
together with its strange crew had voyaged from his homeland. When Cook returned to New Zealand on the second
voyage Maori enquired first after Tupa'ia, whose reputation
had spread far beyond those places he had visited in 1769.
During his months on the *Endeavour*, Tupa'ia clearly regarded
himself as Cook's equal, if not his superior, and when he died
at Batavia on the homeward voyage Cook's rather grudging
obituary was that he was 'a Shrewd Sensible Ingenious Man,
but proud and obstinate, which often made his situation on
board both disagreeable to himself and those about him'.
There is no telling what Tupa'ia on the first voyage and Mai
on the third told their fellow Polynesians about their British
shipboard companions, but one factor in Cook's difficulties
at Lifuka in 1777 seems to have been Mai's insistence that
Cook was not a great chief in his own country.

Even so, it is a sign of the importance of Cook's name and memory that when Bligh in the *Bounty* reached Tahiti in 1788 on his notorious breadfruit voyage he warned his crew that 'no person whatever is to intimate that Captain Cook … is dead'. Unknown to Bligh, mixed signals about Cook had been given by the crew of the merchant ship, *Lady Penrhyn*, when it called at Tahiti four months earlier on its homeward voyage from Botany Bay. The ship's surgeon noted that at Matavai Bay 'the Chiefs came on board & enquired after Tutee (Capt. Cook) we told them that he was alive in Britain, but an old Man.' This story was rather spoilt by a naval lieutenant on board the *Lady Penrhyn* who had been with Cook at Kealakekua Bay, and told the islanders that Cook was dead. A potentially awkward situation was avoided when a member of the crew diverted attention from Cook's fate with his assertion that Bligh was Cook's son.

At Tahiti both islanders and crew clearly regarded their links with Cook as a kind of passport. So when Tu made his way across the island to meet Bligh at Matavai Bay he sent before him Webber's portrait of Cook given to him in 1777, and Bligh responded by having its battered frame repaired. After the mutiny those of the *Bounty*'s crew who returned to Tahiti were not slow to claim their own relationship with Cook. When they asked for cattle they 'made the demand in the name of Captain Cook; a name which operated on the natives like a charm'. Later one of the mutineers, James Morrison, witnessed a sacrificial ceremony centring on the portrait during which, he asserted, the explorer was celebrated as 'Chief of the Air, Earth & Water … Chief from the Beach to the Mountains, over Men, Trees & Cattle, over the Birds of the Air and Fishes of the Sea'. The portrait of Cook was to make one final appearance in the journals, when the *Pandora* arrived at Matavai Bay in March 1791 in pursuit of the *Bounty* mutineers. The *Pandora's* surgeon, James Hamilton, noted that the portrait was presented to all ships' captains on arrival, and it was customary for them to record details of their visit on the back. The portrait, he wrote, was 'held by them in the greatest veneration; and I should not be surprised if, one day or other, divine honours should be paid to it.'

Among the islands long after Cook's ships had been and gone, their visits were recalled in stories and songs. At Tanna in the New Hebrides (Vanuatu) a missionary wrote in the 1840s that the Tannese remembered an incident from Cook's second voyage, seventy years earlier, when one of Cook's men shot a man dead, and was put in irons for doing so. The islander, they argued, must have been responsible for the killing of a chief shortly before Cook arrived, and so his own death was a form of supernatural retribution. In the Marquesas (to follow Greg Dening's reconstruction):

> There is a memory of 'Tuti' (Cook). Strangers always ask about 'Tuti'. This man can show the scars that Tuti's 'thunder' left him. 'Tuti' killed, they remember, that one's brother, this one's father. They can even show the 'nail' – the stanchion of the *Resolution's* gangway – that a man was killed for taking.

Where memory failed, invention might take its place. In *Omoo* (1847) Herman Melville noted that in Tahiti

> it is a curious fact that all these people, young and old, will tell you that they have enjoyed the honour of a personal acquaintance with the great navigator, and if you

listen to them, they will go on and tell anecdotes without end.

A later writer and traveller poked gentle fun at the more extravagant claims about Cook's fame in the Pacific. In 1889 Robert Louis Stevenson met Tem Binoka, the ruler of the tiny atoll of Abemama in the Gilbert Islands (Kiribati), who had heard about Cook from a passing schooner captain. The King was interested, and sought more information, not in the standard reference works, but in the Bible. 'Here he sought long and earnestly … no word of Cook. The inference was obvious; the explorer was a myth.'

3

COOK IN THE COLONIAL AGE

A NEW KIND OF HERO

In matters both practical and spiritual Cook's achievements found ready recognition in the decades after his death. Adam Smith's *Wealth of Nations* was published in the same year that Cook sailed on his last voyage, and to the next generation the explorer seemed a travelling representative of the doctrine expounded in Smith's book as his voyages opened new worlds to British enterprise. It was altogether appropriate that in the 'Navigation' section of James Barry's huge painting, 'The Progress of Human Culture', which stretched across the hall of the London headquarters of the Royal Society of Arts and Manufactures, Cook appeared alongside the more warlike figures of Drake and Raleigh. As Bernard Smith puts it, Cook was 'a new kind of hero for a new time'. This interpretation has its limitations, for the time was not so new that it was not able within twenty years of Cook's death to produce a rather more old-fashioned type of hero, whose fame was to eclipse Cook's. Members of the same service, Horatio Nelson and James Cook had little in common except the respect of their superiors and the affection of their crews. In terms of temperament, personal morality, and professional achievement, the two seamen represented very different strains of national endeavour. The gulf was not unbridgeable, for some saw British naval power as the key to opening the Pacific, and Cook and Nelson as different sides of the same coin. When the evangelically-minded Captain John Erskine, the first Senior Officer of the Navy's Australian Division, sailed for the Pacific in 1840 he had only two portraits in his cabin, Nelson's and Cook's.

During the long wars with France, while in the Pacific explorers, traders and missionaries followed in the wake of Cook, at home his light dimmed before the bright glow of Nelson's battle honours. There could be no greater contrast than that between the national mourning and the ceremonial funeral procession to St Paul's that followed Nelson's death, and the reluctance by government, national or local, to set up a monument to commemorate Cook. The *Gentleman's Magazine* published letters calling for a memorial in Westminster Abbey (1785 and 1789) or in Cleveland (1787 and 1791), and when these suggestions came to nothing put forward a despairing proposal that the Australian continent should be named 'Cookia'. Kippis made the best of a bad job when having regretted that there was no monument to Cook in Westminster Abbey he reassured his readers that the explorer's fame 'stands upon a wider base ... The name of Cook will be held in honour, and received with applause, so long as the records of human events shall continue.' However, when war came to an end in 1815, the focus of British naval exploration moved to the Arctic. It might be going too far to call the woebegone figure of Sir John Franklin a hero, although he may have some claims to a self-inflicted martyrdom; but of public fascination with his last, disastrous voyage and the exploits of his fellow explorers in polar regions there can be no doubt.

Cook's successors in the Pacific had different priorities. In 1795 Thomas Haweis preached a sermon to the newly established London Missionary Society in which he announced that as a result of Cook's voyages, 'A new world hath lately opened to our view ... New Holland, New Zealand, and the innumerable islands, which spot the bosom of the Pacific Ocean.' There, despite the beauty of the environment,

> savage nature still feasts on the flesh of its prisoners – appeases its Gods with human sacrifices – whole socie- ties of men and women live promiscuously, and murder every infant born among them ... No other part of the heathen world, [he concluded] affords so promising a field for a Christian mission.

The sermon was the evangelical reaction to James King's indulgent remarks in his introduction to the third volume of the authorised account of Cook's last voyage:

> Some rays of light must have darted on the Friendly, Society and Sandwich Islands, by our repeated inter- course with them. Convinced by comparing themselves to their English visitors, of their extreme inferiority, they will probably endeavour to emerge from it, to rise nearer to a level with those, who left behind them so many proofs of their generosity and humanity.

In 1796 the missionary vessel *Duff* left for Tahiti, and the following March anchored at Matavai Bay, the place above all in Polynesia made famous by the narratives of Cook and the paintings of Hodges and Webber. Soon Cook's descrip- tions were supplemented by the reports of missionaries whose task it was to save the Pacific islanders from eternal hellfire. To the missionaries and their superiors at home, Cook's voyages were the prelude to the conversion of the Pacific islands. Cheap abridged accounts of his voyages were available in Sunday schools, and were popular reading among Victorian families. They were followed by the beguiling South Seas stories of later writers such as Ballantyne and Stevenson, but the more domesticated scenes of Dickens also had their Cook moments. Rod Edmond has noted that prints showing the death of Cook hung on the walls of rooms in *Great Expectations* and *Bleak House*, while Pet's father in *Little Dorrit* boasted that 'she will be a greater traveller in the course of time than Captain Cook'.

For the pioneers on board the *Duff* and their immediate successors, the volumes of Cook's voyages were required reading, but the next generation of missionaries had its own texts. William Ellis's *Polynesian Researches* (1829) and John Williams's best-selling *Narrative of Missionary Enterprises* (1837) described their efforts in the islands that helped to bring an end to the Polynesian world that Cook had witnessed and described. There were still reminders of Cook wherever the missionaries went. In Hawai'i, where Ellis stayed after years in Tahiti, he spent much time investigating the circumstances of Cook's death. In 1823 he first made 'a pilgrimage' to the rock on the shore of Kealakekua Bay where Cook was killed, and then climbed high on the cliffs above the village of Kaawaloa to the walled enclosure where Cook's body had been dismembered. Other parts of his Hawaiian reports perhaps owe something to wishful thinking. Chiefs wanted to know why the missionaries had not come sooner, asked whether it was their punishment for having killed Cook, and wept over pictures of the death scene.

The killing of John Williams at Eromanga in 1839 brought

17. *The death of John Williams, from Basil Mathews,* John Williams
the Shipbuilder *(1915). The killing of the missionary on the island of
Eromanga in 1839, clubbed down at the water's edge, with his companions
too far away to offer help, bore a striking resemblance to the popular
depictions of the death of Cook.*

back even more poignant memories of Cook's death. It was at Eromanga that Cook had met a hostile reception more than sixty years earlier, and Williams's death there echoed Cook's in Hawai'i as the missionary was clubbed face-down in the water, with help near at hand but not near enough. During his life Williams had compared himself with Cook as he followed the track of the great navigator whose surveys, he wrote, 'you may follow … with as much confidence as you travel the high roads of England'. Describing Rarotonga in the Cook Islands, he noted that, 'This splendid island escaped the untiring researches of Captain Cook, and was discovered by myself.' Just as Cook on his return from his second voyage suspected that the limits of his forthcoming retirement at Greenwich Hospital would be 'far too small for an active mind like mine', so Williams proclaimed, 'I cannot content myself within the narrow limits of a single reef.' The comparison was heightened by the similarities between the deaths of the two men, and in 1842 Williams's biographer, the Revd John Campbell, paid tribute to both men, while making a distinction between their respective achievements:

> The career of the seaman shone resplendent with mari-time, the career of the missionary with moral, glory … the one represented England's power and science, the other her piety and humanity … both were killed by the club of the savage.

At home, Williams became (in the title of Campbell's biography) 'The Martyr of Erromanga'. Sales of his book leapt, and colour prints of his death achieved wide circulation. All in all, it seemed that Williams was 'a better Cook for a religiously awakened public'.

Abridged accounts of Cook's voyages and short biographies of the explorer continued to appear by the dozen, the former mostly based on Kippis, and the latter falling into what Oskar Spate has called the 'Men who made the Empire' type of book. There were some exceptions. In 1836 the Revd George Young, Secretary of the Whitby Literary and Philosophical Society, published *The Life and Voyages of Captain James Cook*. Young stressed that his book was independent of Kippis, and unlike him he made an effort to include local information and reminiscences about the explorer. He also gave short shrift to those who found excuses for the way in which Cook seemingly accepted his role as Lono on Hawai'i. As far as the ceremony at the temple on the first landing went, Young wrote:

> It is much to be regretted, that in this instance, our illustrious countryman suffered his curiosity to overcome his sense of duty. However eager he might be, to know the religious rites of this people he ought not to have shared in their idols. As a Christian he was bound, both to refuse adoration to their gods, and to reject it when offered to himself.

Still more objectionable was the similar ceremony performed a few days later, 'not to speak of the more common tokens of adoration, almost daily offered to him by the priests or the people'. Much later in the century, the noted writer Walter Besant produced *Captain Cook* (1890) for Macmillan's 'Men of Action' series, whose pantheon of heroes included Drake, Clive, Nelson and Wolfe. Besant's approach was critical, especially as far as Cook's last voyage was concerned. Douglas was accused of 'doctoring' Cook's journal, while the 'Cook as Lono' aspect of the voyage met with little approval:

We must conclude that Cook's attitude showed a readiness to accept any honours, provided only that they assisted in victualling his ship and promoting the success of the expedition ... the sequel proved that he would have done better to repudiate these honours.

The death of Cook was described from Hawaiian sources as well as from the more usual British ones, and Besant concluded, 'Thus ended, ingloriously, and as the result of an ill-advised attempt at high-handed justice, the life of the greatest navigator of any age.'

As Besant acknowledged, Cook remained pre-eminent as a navigator, but in a sense he and his contemporaries in the Pacific had been too effective as explorers. In just a few decades they had revealed the main features of the great ocean until there were no more mysteries left. To the reading public the exploitation of exploration would never be as fascinating as first 'discovery', and other regions held more allure. In the Arctic men were pitted against nature in its most extreme forms, while in tropical Africa David Livingstone held the stage as a fearless explorer and as a saviour of peoples subject to the horrors of the Arab slave trade. The centenary of Cook's death in 1879 passed without much notice in Britain, and although the Colonial and Indian Exhibition held in London in 1886 displayed 'A Collection of Relics of the late Captain James Cook', this was included at the request of the government of New South Wales.

OUR COLUMBUS OF THE SOUTH

Whatever the lack of interest in Cook in his own country, in parts of the overseas empire his role took on a new dimension.

During the nineteenth century Cook's weeks on the east coast
of Australia in 1770 became part of a nation-building myth
that ignored not only his Dutch predecessors and the country's Aboriginal inhabitants but also the awkward fact that
Cook himself had never suggested the region as a possible
colony. The explorer's emergence as a founding father began
in low-key fashion in 1822 when the newly-established Philosophical Society of Australia set up a brass plate at Cook's
supposed landing place at Kurnell in Botany Bay. The spot
had been indicated by 'a blackfellow, hoary with age', who
had witnessed the *Endeavour*'s arrival in 1770. Thus guided,
a delegation from the Society went into action:

> Here fix the tablet – this must be the place
> Where our Columbus of the South did land

Later in the century imperially minded colonists working
through such organisations as the Australian Patriotic Association turned to Cook as a more sympathetic progenitor of
white Australia than the austere figure of Arthur Phillip and
his convict fleet. A Cook window was installed in the Great
Hall of Sydney University when it was opened in 1859, while
in 1868 28 April was declared a public holiday since it was
'the anniversary of the landing of Captain Cook and of the
first hoisting of the British flag in Australia'. The centenary
in 1870 of the Botany Bay landing attracted little attention,
although the following year an Australian businessman set
up an obelisk on the shores of the bay (more than a kilometre
from the brass plate of 1822). In 1879 a more imposing monument in the form of a statue of Cook – cast in England, and
shipped out – was unveiled in Hyde Park, Sydney. There was
a large crowd on the day, but the Australian journalist Jillian

18. The Captain Cook Memorial in Hyde Park, Sydney, photograph from 1879, the year of its unveiling.

Robertson has noted that the dignity of the occasion was marred by those 'irreverent souls' who spotted that the tilted telescope held low down by Cook at his left side resembled from the other side of the monument an erect male organ.

The union of the colonies in the Commonwealth of

Australia in 1901 was a key moment in the shaping of the new nation, and the celebrations included a reconstruction of Cook's landing at Botany Bay. There a few Aborigines were scattered by mock musket-fire, while the actor playing Dr Solander shouted after them:

As shadows flee before the dawn of day,
So the dark tribes of Earth in terror flee
Before the white man's ever onward tread;
And all the night of ignorance and sin
Both vanish as the light of Truth's fair day
Dawns in the East and spreads o'er all the Earth.

It was the only reference to the original Aboriginal inhabitants of Botany Bay in twelve pages of poetic declamation.

The twentieth century saw the development of a cult in which Cook, the self-made man of humble beginnings, represented the pioneering virtues of the new nation. The cult began in the classroom, where school texts began their history of Australia with Cook's voyages. By the end there were Cook monuments, Cook playing fields, Cook fountains, Cook hotels and restaurants, Cook stamps, a James Cook University, and even a small house built by Cook's father long after his son left home which was shipped at great expense from Yorkshire to Australia. There in its new location in Melbourne's botanical gardens it was long and wrongly described as Cook's Cottage before it was more correctly named Cooks' Cottage. There was something odd about this devotion to a British hero at a time when Australia was moving away in terms of material and sentimental ties from Britain. One of Gail Morgan's characters in her novel *Patent Lies* explains that, as far as Australia was concerned, 'historically [Cook] did little more than draw up a decent map, but history does not always matter'. For many Australians, Cook discovered Australia. As the 1822 plate at Kurnell proclaimed, he was their Columbus; the fact that the Dutch had charted two-thirds of the Australian coastline more than a century earlier seemed not to count. Hence the excitement when every few years a book appears that challenges Cook's assumed priority with an earlier 'discoverer' from among an ever-growing group of Portuguese, Spanish, French and Chinese navigators. The Australian newspaper headlines that greeted the most recent of these books, Peter Trickett's *Beyond Capricorn* (2007), are self-revelatory: 'Another nail in Cook's coffin'; 'New doubts that Cook discovered Australia'; 'Captain Cook scuppered by book'.

A similar pattern can be seen in the British settlement of New Zealand. Here Cook's unique status is more understandable. His magnificent coastal survey of New Zealand on his first voyage put the country on the map in a quite literal way. For the first time the now-familiar shape of the twin islands appeared, while Cook's journal entries and the paintings of his artists depicted a country whose inhabitants and flora and fauna were totally unknown to Europeans. His charts, many used until well into the nineteenth century, named hundreds of prominent geographical features that became familiar to later settlers. Cook even selected the areas he thought would be best suited to future British settlement – the Bay of Islands and the Waihou River (the latter auspiciously named by Cook the Thames). And as in Australia, Cook's sturdy, unassuming virtues fitted New Zealanders' rugged perspectives of themselves. Again, as in early Australia, there was a lack of alternative founding fathers – no other explorer to match him, no war of independence to produce a George Washington, and in the country's days as a colony few charismatic political leaders.

HE DIED BY THE VISITATION OF GOD

Far away from Britain's developing colonies of white settlement in the South Pacific, different interpretations of Cook were taking shape in Hawai'i. While visitors to Kealakekua Bay continued to pay their respects to the memory of Cook, elsewhere in the Hawaiian group more hostile attitudes emerged as American traders and missionaries jostled with their British counterparts for positions of influence. The first American missionaries arrived in Hawai'i in 1820, the year after Kamehameha II (Liholilo, the son of Kamehameha I), abolished the traditional culture system of gods, idols and *tabu* that had dominated the island at the time of Cook's visit. By the mid-1820s the Hawaiian royal family had converted to Christianity, which became the new state religion. Political rather than spiritual reasons accounted for this dramatic change, but the missionaries quickly took advantage of the new opportunities that opened up. By the 1830s a trickle of conversions had increased to a flood, and mission schools staffed by Hawaiian teachers trained by the missionaries were instructing their pupils in reading, writing, and the elements of Christianity.

In time, American visitors – missionaries and others – would sift Hawaiian oral traditions to provide an indigenous history of the islands; but the first attempt was made by the English missionary, William Ellis, who gave an emotional account of visiting Kealakekua Bay in his *Narrative of a Tour through Hawaii* (1826). His *Polynesian Researches* (1829) a few years later dug more deeply into Hawaiian reactions to Cook, and produced a version which in effect founded the 'Cook as Lono' interpretation. In his *Narrative* Ellis printed what he was told about the treatment of Cook's remains, although how far this apparently first-hand account was an accurate transcription of oral testimony is uncertain:

> After he was dead, we all wailed. His bones were separated – the flesh was scraped off and burnt, as was the practice in regard to our own chiefs when they died. We thought he was the god Rono, worshipped him as such and after his death reverenced his bones ...

As they did other items associated with Cook, including a sledge from the northwest coast of America that had been left ashore at Kealakekua Bay. In his later book Ellis added more detail. Rono or Lono was a king or chief from an earlier age who fled Hawai'i after killing his wife, and sailed 'in a singularly shaped canoe' to a distant land. When Cook arrived at Kealakekua Bay it was supposed that he was Rono returned, until 'in the attacks made upon him, they saw his blood running, and heard his groans, they said, "No, this is not Rono"'.

In the 1830s a more elaborate attempt was made by an American missionary, the Revd Sheldon Dibble, to record Hawaiian recollections of their earlier history by using the services of his students at the missionary seminary of Lahainaluna on Maui. He considered it unacceptable that his students 'whilst they were becoming acquainted with other nations, should remain to a great degree in ignorance of their own'. He described his investigating methods as follows:

I first made out a list of questions ... I then selected ten of
the best scholars of the Seminary, and formed them into a
class of inquiry ... I then requested them to go individu-
ally and separately to the oldest and most knowing of the
chiefs and people ... At the time of meeting each scholar
read what he has written – discrepancies were reconciled
and corrections made by each other [made by himself,
Dibble wrote in the original Hawaiian edition], and then
all the compositions were handed to me, out of which I
managed to make one connected and true account.

The process, with its novice questioners, modifications of
original statements, and final synthesis by Dibble, an evangelical Christian, hardly conforms to today's best practice;
but the *Mooolelo Hawaii* (printed in Hawaiian in 1838) and
its subsequent English-language editions retrieved a great
deal of indigenous evidence that otherwise would have been
lost. In the words of Herb Kawainui Kane, Dibble's text was
'studied by generations of Hawaiian students [and] infected
Hawaiians with a dislike of Cook that persists today'.

Dibble, a member of the American Board of Commis-
sioners for Foreign Missions, was strenuously opposed to
the British presence in Hawai'i, and claimed that his investigations showed that Cook was an idolater and a bringer of
venereal disease. He began the story of Cook in the islands
with the expedition's first brief stay at Kauai in January 1778
when Dibble claimed that the firing of the ships' cannon
and a firework display filled the people with 'confusion and
terror'. They were convinced that the strangers were 'superior
beings', and that their leader was a god called Lono, one of
their 'most venerated gods', who had gone to a distant land,
and had now returned. In reality, Dibble lamented, it was a

disastrous moment in Hawaiian history, for 'here and at this time, in the form of a loathsome disease, was dug the grave of the Hawaiian nation'. And far from trying to prevent the spread of venereal disease Cook encouraged the excesses of his crew by taking as his sexual partner a Kauai princess, Lelemahoalani.

The shipboard records of this first known visit by a European ship to any of the Hawaiian Islands tell a different and rather more complicated story as far as Cook's actions were concerned. There was no firing of the ships' great guns, and no firework display. On the fundamental issue of venereal disease Cook (like his immediate European predecessors in the Pacific, Wallis and Bougainville) did his utmost to prevent its spread among the Pacific islands. Men were inspected by the surgeons before they were allowed ashore, attempts were made to control the women coming on board – but all to no avail. British and French blamed each other; and the dispute was confused by the similarity between yaws, indigenous to the Pacific, and syphilis. By the later stages of his third voyage Cook was vastly experienced, and vastly disillusioned, in attempts to control venereal disease. As he sent boats ashore on Kauai on 20 January 1778 he wrote a long and reflective entry in his journal:

As there were some venereal complaints on both the Ships, in order to prevent its being communicated to these people, I gave orders that no Women, on any account whatever were to be admitted on board the Ships, I also forbid all manner of connection with them, and ordered that none who had the venereal upon them should go out of the ships. But whether these regulations had the desired effect or no time can only discover. It is no more

than what I did when I first visited the Friendly [Tonga]
Islands yet I afterward found it did not succeed, and I am
much afraid this will always be the case where it is necessary to have a number of people on shore; the opportunities and inducements to an intercourse between the
sex, are there too many to be guarded against. It is also a
doubt with me whether the most skilfull of the [medical]
Faculty can tell whether every man who has had the
venereal is so far cured as not to communicate it further,
I think I could mention some instances to the contrary. It
is likewise well known that amongst a number of men,
there will be found some who will endeavour to conceal
this disorder, and there are some again who care not to
whom they communicate it ...

Other journals testify to the seriousness with which this
prohibition was enforced; men were flogged with a dozen or
two dozen lashes for trying to evade it. But the task was an
impossible one, as Cook suspected. On shore eager women
'used all their Arts' to entice crew into their dwellings. 'They
were so importunate that they absolutely would take no
denial,' wrote Samwell. For their part, some seamen dressed
their chosen partners in men's clothes in order to smuggle
them on board the ships. And then, on 30 January, Cook
wrote, 'The very thing happened that I had above all others
wished to prevent.' Lieutenant Gore and twenty men were
ashore trading for provisions, but were unable to return to
the ship because of the high surf, and were forced to remain
– some very willingly, no doubt – among the local populace
for two days.

As the ships returned to Hawaiian waters in late 1778
Cook again issued orders forbidding women to come on

board the ships, and prohibiting any of the crew with symp-
toms of venereal disease from going on shore. On both the
Resolution and the *Discovery* a list of those suspected of
having the disease was displayed on the quarter-deck. The
order was issued on 28 November as the ships approached
Maui, but an entry in Lieutenant King's journal the same
day showed that it was too late. Canoes came alongside the
ships with women trying to come on board who 'abusd &
ridiculed us' when they were kept away. Sadly, there were
other demands:

> Three of the Natives have apply'd to us, for help in their
> great distress: they had a Clap, their Penis was much
> swell'd, & inflamed. The manner in which these innocent
> People complained to us, seemd to me to shew that they
> consider'd us as the Original authors.

Some on board the ships were doubtful whether the disease
could have spread in less than a year from Kauai, more than
200 miles distant, and wondered whether a Spanish ship was
responsible. Samwell thought that the disease was 'pretty
universal' among the islanders before the ships' arrival, but
Cook never seems to have been in any doubt that his own
men were guilty. 'I as yet knew of no other way they [the
islanders] could come by it,' he wrote, and when the ships
returned to Kauai the following March, King confirmed his
dead captain's opinion:

> One man…told us that we had left a disorder amongst
> their Women, which had killd several of them as well as
> Men; he himself was infectd with the Venereal disease,
> & describ'd in feeling terms the havock it had made, &

its pains &c. I was never more thoroughly Satisfyd of a doubtful point than from this Circumstance, that we were the Authors of this disease in this Place.

Dibble's horror at the introduction of the 'loathsome disease' to the Hawaiian Islands was matched by Cook's officers – 'an everlasting and Miserable plague' (Riou); 'that dreadful distemper' (Edgar); 'that greatest plague that ever the human Race was afflicted with' (Samwell). Where the two sides parted company was on the question of Cook's personal behaviour. At no time on his voyages is there any evidence that Cook had sexual relations with the women he encountered; and there were plenty of sharp-eyed observers on the ships who would have noticed, and mentioned, the fact if he had. And his alleged relationship with Lelemahoalani on Kauai is made even more unlikely since genealogical research has shown that she was only eight at the time.

Dibble's book became a foundation text for generations of Hawaiian scholars. One of the most influential of these was David Malo, who as a mature student joined Dibble at the Lahainaluna school in the 1830s and helped him to collect material for the *Mooolelo Hawaii*. His own researches into Hawaiian history were eventually translated into English, and published as *Hawaiian Antiquities* in 1903. A central chapter in the book was 'Concerning the Makahiki', which threw much new light on the identification of Cook as Lono. Malo explained that the four months of the Makahiki season, from November to early February, were a time of pleasure and leisure. Each year an image of the Makahiki god was made in the form of a stick of wood with a carved figure at the top decorated with white *tapa* (bark) cloth. A cross-piece was tied to the neck of the figure, from which hung bird feathers and skins. The figure processed around the island in a clockwise direction, always keeping the interior to its right. On its journey hogs and other foodstuffs were presented to the god and its attendants, and after it was received by the King then the people rejoiced by engaging in boxing matches and other games. Malo concluded, 'Captain Cook was named Lono after this god, because of the resemblance the sails of his ship bore to the tapa of the god.' In time, Malo's brief comment would be extended into a fully-fledged interpretation of Cook's reception in Hawai'i.

Another of Dibble's students was S.M. Kamakau, who entered the Lahainaluna school at the age of seventeen and probably helped with the compiling of the *Mooolelo Hawaii*. In time, he became one of the most widely-read Hawaiian writers of the period, publishing a series of articles on Hawaiian history in weekly newspapers between 1866 and 1871. Again, there was much on the Makahiki festival and Lono, together with stories that shortly before Cook's arrival there were prophecies of the arrival of the *haole* or foreigner. Cook was taken to be Lono, 'worshipped with great reverence' until the day of his death, when in the fracas a chief wounded by Cook

> seized Lono with his strong hand and held him fast, but did not kill him because he thought he could not kill a god. But when Lono cried out and fell, [the chief] thought he was human ... then he struck Lono and killed him.

More influential outside Hawai'i were the books written by American visitors to the islands and published in the United States. Although largely based on *Mooolelo Hawaii* and other local sources, they had their own agenda, one which was

to varying degrees hostile to Britain and its agents. Hiram
Bingham, the unofficial leader of the American missionaries,
lived for more than twenty years in the islands before publishing an account of his experiences. He had no doubt that
Cook's death was the result of his

> direct encouragement of idolatry, and especially for his
> audacity in allowing himself like the proud and magiste-
> rial Herod to be idolized, he was left to infatuation and
> died by the visitation of God.

Another American, James J. Jarves, spent four years in
Hawai'i as editor of a weekly Honolulu paper, *The Polynesian*,
and on his return to the United States published a *History
of the Hawaiian or Sandwich Islands*. It displayed an almost
obsessive concern to depict Cook in the worst possible light,
and relied heavily on Ledyard's account of Cook's stay in
Hawai'i. Here once more was the story of the princess at
Kauai forced to sleep with Cook, embellished with fictitious
detail about the terrifying effect of the firing of the ships'
cannon. A year later, as Cook landed at Kealakekua Bay,
Jarves had no doubts about the significance of his behaviour
at the temple near the beach:

> It seems impossible that any one in the least acquainted
> with the customs of Polynesia, could for a moment
> have doubted that all this form was intended for ado-
> ration ... the natives say that Cook performed his part
> in the heathen farce, without the slightest opposition.
> The numerous offerings, the idols and temples to which
> he was borne, the long prayers, recitations and chants
> addressed to him, must have carried conviction to his

mind that it was intended solely for religious homage, and the whole form a species of deification or consecration of himself.

Appealing to a different reading public were the writings of Mark Twain, whose visit to the islands in 1866 resulted in a series of newspaper articles and popular lectures, and a book, *Roughing It*. Taking his lead from Ledyard and Jarves, Twain recounted the story of how Cook was assumed by the Hawaiian people to be their god Lono, and took advantage of this to extract huge quantities of provisions without payment. Following Kamakau's version, Twain wrote how on the day of his death Cook shot two men before being held down by a chief in a grip so strong that he groaned:

> It was his death warrant. The fraud which had served him so well was discovered at last. The natives shouted, 'He groaned – he is not a god' and instantly they fell upon him and killed him.

It was, Twain considered, 'justifiable homicide'.

In 1874 a group of patriotic British citizens living in Hawai'i expressed their own point of view when they erected a concrete monument to Cook at Kealakekua Bay. Three years later it was replaced by a more imposing obelisk, which was surrounded by a chain fence suspended between a dozen upturned muzzle-loading cannon brought ashore from a British warship. The cannon have long since gone, but the obelisk still stands, periodically repainted and cleaned of graffiti by Royal Navy seamen. An indication of a more radical local sentiment came with the centenary in 1878 of Cook's first arrival in the Islands. The Hawaiian legislature approved the erection of a statue in Honolulu to mark the occasion, but it was not of Cook but of Kamehameha I, who as a young chief was reported to have been involved in the attack of 14 February. Native Hawaiian opinion of Cook at this time was later summed up by John Stokes, the Australian-born Curator of the Bernice P. Bishop Museum in Honolulu:

> He was an arch-fiend, a blasphemer, a libertine, a conscienceless adventurer and the murderer of the Hawaiian race through the introduction and communication of venereal disease, who came to a violent end by means of the avenging agency of the Almighty.

It was a minority view, not held and not widely known outside Hawai'i, but it contained the seeds of a very different interpretation of Cook from that generally accepted in the English-speaking world.

Fifty years later, in 1928, a more conventional note was struck at the sesquicentennial celebrations sponsored by the Hawaiian Historical Society. By now the islands were under American rule, for the Hawaiian monarchy had been overthrown in 1893, and the islands were annexed by the United States five years later. There were ceremonies and speeches at Kauai, Honolulu, and Kealakekua Bay, where British, Australian and New Zealand cruisers, and an American battleship, anchored offshore. A bronze tablet was unveiled on the rock where it was supposed that Cook was killed, while another set up in Honolulu proclaimed that Cook was the 'Forerunner of Modern Civilization in the Pacific Ocean'. Prominent in the speech-making at the various celebrations was the veteran Australian politician, Sir Joseph Carruthers, former premier of New South Wales, whose letter to *The Times* in 1908 had helped to bring about the placing of a statue of Cook near the old Admiralty building in the Mall – a belated commemoration, one might think. Predictably, his version of Cook's stay in Hawai'i had no truck with stories of Lono. And in Honolulu the Governor, Wallace R. Farrington, gave an address which, even in 1928, might have seemed patronising as he lamented the barbaric way in which a 'benighted people' had killed 'the great Explorer'. More moderately, the *Honolulu Advertiser* editorialised on 13 August 1928: 'A century and a half ago Captain James Cook unlocked the isolation which had shrouded the Hawaiian people in a veil of silence,' and in an official booklet the views of Carruthers and Farrington were balanced by Kamakau's version of the death of Cook, written in 1867.

It was perhaps this last that persuaded Carruthers, infuriated by the way in which 'the memory of Captain Cook has been besmirched by narrow-minded men', to publish a full-length defence of Cook in 1930. He had been irritated on his first visit to the Hawaiian Islands in 1924 when his remarks in praise of the explorer were interrupted by 'a prominent citizen of Honolulu', who told him that 'Cook and his crews behaved badly, committed great excesses contributing to his death and left behind a trail of evil'. In his book Carruthers produced a benign interpretation of Cook's stay on Hawai'i that differed little from that first presented in Douglas's authorised account of 1784. Cook's death came about through a series of unfortunate misunderstandings, and he gave his life to save those of others. 'That is how Captain Cook died. Brave as a lion to the last, but withal prompted by his humane instincts to prevent bloodshed.'

4

COOK IN A POSTCOLONIAL WORLD

ONE MIGHT ASK IF THERE IS ANYTHING ELSE TO SAY

In 1934 the New Zealand scholar, J.C. Beaglehole, then in his early thirties, made a decision that was to have a far-reaching effect on the standing of Captain Cook. After his *Exploration of the Pacific* was published in that year Beaglehole decided that it was time for a new life of Cook, based on the original manuscript journals, and that as a preliminary he would publish those journals in comprehensive, critical editions. The 'preliminary' was to be his life's work. It was only well after the Second World War that one by one the mighty volumes appeared, in 1955, 1961 and 1967, 3,359 pages in all, heavily annotated, to be followed by the long-awaited biography, published in 1974, three years after Beaglehole's death. For the first time, scholars had to hand what Cook had actually written, with his journal entries shown in all their variant forms, rather than the polite versions produced by his eighteenth-century editors. The long introductions to the volumes were books in their own right, while Beaglehole's sympathetic biography – another 760 pages – so massive, so authoritative, was surely the last word on Cook. As the editors of a volume of conference papers on Cook put it, 'Having read Beaglehole, one might ask if there is anything else to say.' In fact, Beaglehole's devoted work marked the beginning of a new stage in Cook scholarship, much of which opened up very different paths from those he had followed.

At the same time as Beaglehole was working on Cook's journals another scholar was looking at the voyages from a rather different perspective. In 1960 Bernard Smith published his *European Vision and the South Pacific*, a book that had an influence on several different scholarly areas. Art and science were Smith's preoccupations. In the chapters on Cook's voyages Banks and the Forsters, Hodges and Webber, dominated. Smith's order of priorities was shown when he wrote that it was 'widely held by naturalists and writers that Cook's scientists, *aided by his seamen* [my italics], would gradually complete the picture of the universe'. Whereas one feels that for Beaglehole the 'supernumeraries' were always subordinate, and could sometimes be irritating nuisances, in Smith's pages they are an important part of a genuine collaborative enterprise.

One of the first popular attempts to build on the developing Cook scholarship was Alan Moorehead's best-selling *The Fatal Impact: An Account of the Invasion of the South Pacific*. In his author's note Moorehead explained:

I have concentrated upon one aspect of Cook's voyages, namely that fateful moment when a social capsule is broken into, when primitive creatures, beasts as well as men, are confronted for the first time with civilization.

Tahiti is the focal point of almost half the book, and in apocalyptic terms it described the effect of explorers and their followers on 'the slow, natural rhythm of life on the island as it had been lived till then'. It was, although Moorehead did not much acknowledge the fact, an elaboration of a thesis about the Pacific voyages that had been present from the beginning. Moorehead's book was published in 1966, only a few years before the current obsession with centennials, bicentennials and every other kind of anniversary fastened on Cook. There were to be conferences and publications, ceremonies and re-enactments, and finally the accolade that placed Cook along-side Columbus and Drake on the world stage, the building of a full-size replica of his first Pacific command, HM Bark *Endeavour*. Anniversaries of this sort have their own momen-tum and rationale: commercial, educational, patriotic. It is difficult for them to be anything but celebratory, although 1992, Columbus Year, with its controversies in the United States and far beyond, was to change that.

The various bicentennials of Cook's voyages were marked by an impressive output of new work, although until the bicentennial of the third voyage most publications supple-mented rather than challenged Beaglehole's interpretation. The change came in the 1978 conference held in Vancouver to commemorate the two-hundredth anniversary of Cook's arrival on the northwest coast of America. The impact of the voyages was seen to be more far-reaching than ever, but the emphasis on the first-person singular that had survived from Douglas to Beaglehole faded in favour of an interpreta-tion that gave weight to the collective achievement of Cook and his companions. So there were papers on Banks, Dal-rymple and the Forsters, while a critical summation of the antiscorbutic methods followed by Cook as being 'a blun-derbuss approach' lent support to the view that his achieve-ment in combating scurvy had perhaps been overstated. Even Cook's competence as an explorer on his third voyage was called into question. Little wonder that the editors of the conference volume, *Captain Cook and His Times*, found it necessary to display immediately after the title page Bernard Smith's remark at the conference: 'It has not been part of my intention to discredit the achievements of Cook.' And a reminder of another viewpoint came with the refusal of the Nuu-chah-nulth Tribal Council to allow a boatload of Cook enthusiasts from the conference to land at Nootka Sound on Vancouver Island because of their failure to seek prior permission.

As the 1970s gave way to the 1980s the old anticolonialism gave way to postcolonialism. Edward Said held sway for one hemisphere, and in the Americas a new generation of scholars looked afresh at indigenous societies before and during the European arrival. The titles of their works – *The Invasion of America; Stolen Continents; A Long and Terrible Shadow* – indicated a trend which culminated in the furore over the 1992 Columbus celebrations. In the South Pacific similar controversies arose as commemorations took place. Plans in Australia to mark the bicentennial of the arrival of the First Fleet in 1788 met resistance from Aboriginal groups, who saw nothing to celebrate in the beginning of a process that led to the degradation and disappearance of many of their people. To them Australia Day was Invasion Day, commemorated in 1988 by the Long March of Freedom, Justice and Hope through the streets of Sydney. Demonstrations and rallies were accompanied by the refusal of Aboriginal scholars to participate in conferences and books that were associated with the bicentennial. A few years later a reissue of a collection of Bernard Smith's Pacific essays was greeted by one reviewer with the dismissive comment, published two days before Columbus Day 1992, 'It is time for people whose business it is to write history, to present real accounts of Europe's sanguinary exploits in the previously peaceful waters of the Pacific.'

The completion at Fremantle in 1994 of a full-size replica of the *Endeavour* and the vessel's subsequent cruises around the coasts of Australia and New Zealand (before venturing further afield) brought fears of demonstrations. In the event, protests were muted, and the replica's visit to Turanganui (Poverty Bay), where a Maori chief had been shot dead by Cook's men in 1769, passed without violence except to a statue of Cook. There, as elsewhere, Maori representatives complained that 'when a Maori event was celebrated it was not accorded the same level of publicity as Pakeha [white] celebrations, leaving the public with only one side of the story'. This theme was taken up by others involved with the replica's visit, who urged that it should be treated as an occasion for reconciliation rather than confrontation. At a service at Anaura Bay in January 1996, Anne Salmond pointed out that meetings between the *Endeavour*'s crew and Maori at Anaura and Uawa had been 'peaceful and untroubled'. In efforts to respect sensitivities there has been some restoration of Maori place-names, and when in 1997 stamps were issued to commemorate six navigators important in the country's early history a careful balance was struck: two Polynesian names, two French, one Dutch, and one British (Cook, of course). At Ship Cove (Meretoto) the Cook monument, gleaming white in its new paint, is now set against Maori carved posts, with a symbolic bridge linking the two cultures.

RETURN TO KEALAKEKUA BAY

The rise of popular interest in Cook during the 1990s was

accompanied by an explosive interplay between academic scholarship and nationalist feelings that centred on Cook's death in Hawai'i. What might have been thought, two hundred years after the event, to be a matter of only antiquarian interest, became a hotly contested issue. Beaglehole in his edition of the records of Cook's third voyage had given some attention to the thesis that the Hawaiians regarded Cook as a god, but thought that the acts of prostration and apparent worship at Kealakekua Bay did not amount to conclusive evidence of deification. In his posthumous biography of Cook he moved closer towards accepting that the Hawaiians had moved from veneration to adoration, but at the time of writing had presumably not been able to consider Gavan Daws' interpretation of Cook in Hawai'i, not simply as a god but, crucially, as a flawed god. Daws made much of the tensions between the Lono priests of the temple of Hikiau and the warrior chiefs of Kaawaloa who followed Ku. He speculated that on 14 February the chiefs defended Kalani'opu'u against the aggressive actions 'of a god who might very well not be a god, and whose period of ascendancy was in any case drawing to an end'. Beaglehole rather emphasised the practical problems of a commander who at times seemed near the end of his tether, distracted and infuriated by the setbacks of the voyage, and above all by the incessant stealing in the islands. His thesis is clear. Cook started the voyage a tired man, and the further strains of the voyage blunted his reactions, until on 14 February 1779 with 'his patience tried beyond its limit', he acted with far less than his usual judgement of situations. 'At the fatal moment,' Beaglehole wrote, 'the strained cord snapped.'

There the matter rested until the arrival on the scene of the distinguished Chicago anthropologist, Marshall Sahlins, who argued that the sequence of events in Hawai'i in the late winter of 1778–9 could only be understood in the context of the acceptance by the Hawaiians of Cook as the god Lono. Using the shipboard journals and the later Hawaiian records collected by Sheldon Dibble and others, Sahlins showed that Cook had fulfilled all the criteria for Lono, whose voyage each year was celebrated in the Makahiki season (November to early February). He came with the rising of the Pleiades, and left with their setting. To mark his arrival his symbol, a wooden crosspiece festooned with the skins of birds and supporting long strips of white *tapa* cloth, was processed around the island in a clockwise direction. The processing was marked by ceremonies and offerings, and it ended at Kealakekua Bay, 'the path of the gods', at the *heiau* on the beach. So, Cook unwittingly acted out an Hawaiian ritual as his ships, with their white sails hanging from the cross-yards, made their slow clockwise cruise around the island in the Makahiki season, to land at the ordained spot where many thousands of people were waiting for them. Sahlins pointed out that much now fell into place – not only Cook's initial reception, but also the growing anxiety about when he was leaving. Makahiki ended in early February, and it was at the beginning of the month that Cook's officers recorded urgent queries from Kalani'opu'u and the chiefs about their date of departure. As it was, Cook left at roughly the time when he should, the time when each year Lono's canoe was set adrift, and promised to return the next year. When he came back a few days later he was out of season, out of character. Lono had come back at the time of Ku. Three days later, as Cook landed to take Kalani'opu'u hostage, came 'the climactic ritual battle, but played in reverse … the god Lono was wading ashore with his warriors to attack the king'.

Sahlins' interpretation incorporated the view from the shore rather than from the ship and as such had a wide appeal, although it did not go entirely unchallenged. Oskar Spate, for example, wondered whether Sahlins had perhaps fallen into 'an unwarranted cultural determinism'. Such queries were overshadowed by the assault on Sahlins by a fellow anthropologist, the Sri Lankan Gananath Obeyesekere, who in his book, *The Apotheosis of Captain Cook*, condemned the idealisation of Cook, the humane and enlightened explorer, as an exercise in imperial myth-making. He raised a whole series of objections to Sahlins' thesis: the difficulty after more than two hundred years of matching the Hawaiian lunar and the English Gregorian calendars to give precise dates for the Makahiki season in 1779; the improbability that the Hawaiians would accept a British naval officer as a Polynesian god or mistake his heavy three-masted ship for Lono's canoe; the difference between Lono's ritual circuit, on land, and Cook's track, at sea; the discrepancy between Lono, the benign god of fertility, and Cook and his sickly crews. Above all, Obeyesekere attacked Sahlins' reliance on Hawaiian sources collected many years later, and sifted by missionaries, as being 'endemic to the scholarship pertaining to nonliterate peoples who cannot strike back'. The identification of Cook as Lono was a European construct, 'fundamentally based on the Western idea of the redoubtable European who is a god to savage peoples'. Obeyesekere saw the events of 1779 rather in the context of inter-island warfare, and argued that Cook was installed as a high Hawaiian chief, named after but not as Lono, in order to enlist his support in the war against Maui. This alliance Cook wrecked by his unpredictable and violent behaviour, which culminated in his armed incursions ashore after his return to Kealakekua Bay.

Sahlins responded to Obeyesekere's attack with a full-length book in which he accused his critic of 'a pure negation of anthropological knowledge', and of leaving the Hawaiian people with 'a fictional history and a pidgin ethnography'. Away from the bad-tempered wrestling match between the two anthropologists, a strenuous debate opened among Pacific scholars. Much attention focused on the cultural and linguistic problems involved in the crude translation of the Hawaiian *akua* or Tahitian *atua* as 'god' in a Judaic/Christian sense. Greg Dening pointed out that in Polynesia *akua/atua* could refer to wooden statues, birds, sharks, chiefs and sorcerers. To incorporate a powerful visitor into this pantheon would not be surprising, and there are parallels elsewhere in the Pacific, especially in Melanesia. It could be seen as cultural appropriation on Polynesian terms.

The rival interpretations of Sahlins and Obeyeskere, stimulating though they are, both develop fault lines when measured against the chronology of events. Obeyeskere argued that Cook was installed as Lono, not the god but an honorary Hawaiian chief, as part of Kalani'opu'u's strategy to attract Cook and his armaments to his side in the war against Maui. The installation ceremony was carried out under priestly direction on the day of the ships' arrival at Kealakekua Bay. Neither the King nor his high priest, Kauu, was present, and from a reference a few days later to their landing on the island they seem not to have been on Hawai'i at all. They did not appear at Kealakekua Bay until 25 January, more than a week after the ships' arrival, and it is difficult to see how their absence fits with the strategy put forward by Obeyesekere unless we assume a much greater devolution of power than seems likely. In the events leading to Cook's death it is instructive to look at his unexpected return to Kealakekua

COOK IN A POSTCOLONIAL WORLD 163

Bay stripped of the 'god out of season' thesis. Something more mundane seems to be happening than Sahlins' suggestion of ritual inversion. The few journals that refer to the meeting between Cook and Kalani'opu'u on board the *Endeavour* agree that the King was worried, perhaps angry, at the ships' return. To Sahlins this is evidence that

> Cook's return out of season would be sinister to the ruling chiefs because it presented a mirror image of Makahiki politics. Bringing the god ashore during the triumph of the king could reopen the whole question of sovereignty.

However, other alternatives are likely: the strain on food supplies, the disruption of normal life by the presence of so many strangers, and the fear (noted in several journals) that they intended to seize the country.

What happened on 14 February is susceptible of explanations other than Sahlin's thesis of 'a climactic ritual battle'. Cook was not attacked when he landed, either on the 13th , when he chased a supposed thief far inland, or on the 14th. There was no resistance when Cook came ashore with his marines that morning, nor when he arrived at the King's sleeping quarters, nor indeed when he began leading him towards the beach. Samwell's narrative is among the sources that are definite on this point: 'Thus far matters appeared in a favourable train and the natives did not seem much alarmed or apprehensive.' The events that followed: the uneasiness that grew among the swelling crowd of Hawaiians when they saw their king being manhandled as he slumped to the ground, the screams of his wife, the news of the killing of the chief across the bay, the failure of Cook's small-shot to make any impact, need no Lono-style explanations. The sequence of events at Kealakekua Bay on 14 February 1779 that resulted in a score of deaths could have happened on almost any beach during any of Cook's Pacific voyages.

TOO MANY CAPTAIN COOKS

Few of today's scholars indulge in traditional exploration history with its narratives of intrepid pioneers discovering the unknown. Equally, many deplore the way in which accounts of the contact experience tend to be written in terms of a clash of opposites, in which the meeting of different cultures invariably results in violence. The once-fashionable 'Fatal Impact' thesis now has many critics, who point to its patronising tendencies in regarding the Pacific peoples as helpless victims. Much of this will be familiar to those who study the contact process in other parts of the world, but what is unique to the Pacific is the status of 'the beach'. In one sense this was a well-defined physical entity, a boundary separating land and water; in another it was a more tenuous area, sometimes a zone of confrontation and conflict, but also a space where willing intercourse, commercial and sexual, took place.

A continuing problem is the limited extent to which such reinterpretations percolate through to popular writing and presentation. Recognition of Captain Cook, at least at a certain level, is worldwide. Philatelists put together whole albums of stamps showing Cook or his ships, including some issued by countries such as Hungary and Mali that have no coastline. Dozens of statues of Cook or dedicatory monuments mark spots where he landed. Sir Thomas Brock's imposing statue of the explorer unveiled in Whitby in 1914 has

19. Statue of Captain Cook at Cape Schmidt, Chukotka, designed and erected by Yuri Dunaev, c. 1990.

replicas in Alaska (Anchorage), Canada (Victoria), Australia (Melbourne), and the Hawaiian Islands (Kauai). Botany Bay has no fewer than eleven monuments of different shapes and sizes commemorating Cook's landing of April 1770; even so, in 2006 the Australian government announced a competition to design a new monument 'befitting the site that witnessed the first recorded contact between Britain and eastern Indigenous Australians ... the birthplace of a nation'. One of the most extraordinary of all Cook memorials is a towering cast-iron affair at Cape Schmidt (formerly North Cape), near the small Arctic settlement of Chukotka. This was built single-handedly at his own expense by Yuri Dunaev, the air-traffic controller at the local airport. Marine archaeologists search for the remains of the *Endeavour* and *Resolution* in the silt of Newport Harbor, Rhode Island, where they ended their days as transports in the War of American Independence – so far without much result. Some of the uses of Cook's name are clearly appropriate. Britain's new Royal Research Ship is named the *James Cook*, replacing the *Charles Darwin*. Most of the streets, parks and hotels named after Cook are in countries that have some connection with him; but it is less easy to account for the Kapitan Cook restaurant in Gdynia, Poland. Even more unexpected was the revelation in one of Colin Dexter's 'Inspector Morse' novels that the elusive first name of his fictional policeman was 'Endeavour'. Morse's father, it transpired, was a Captain Cook enthusiast.

Relics of Cook fetch high prices at auctions, even though their provenance is often doubtful. In 2003 'The spear that killed Cook' (a newspaper heading) was put up for auction in Edinburgh with an estimate of between £2,000 and £19,000. In the event it was sold for £135,000. Although many of the Hawaiians on the day of Cook's death were armed with spears, there is no record that he was struck by one – clubs, stones and iron daggers are the weapons mentioned. This particular spear was supposedly picked up from the beach at Kealakekua Bay by William Bligh, but since he was not a member of the party that landed with Cook any retrieval must have been on a later occasion. Nor was the spear kept in its original condition, but at some stage was made into a gold-topped walking stick. Even so, the combination of the names of Cook and Bligh was obviously irresistible to the many collectors bidding for the item. Even more bizarre is the story of 'King Kamehameha's Arrow'. This was thought to have been left in London in 1824 by King Kamehameha II on his ill-fated visit to England. The foreshaft of the arrow was made, so it was claimed, from Cook's leg-bone. Since Cook's body was dismembered after his death, and some of his bones were processed around the island for years after, there was nothing inherently improbable about the story; but in 2004 Australian investigators reported that DNA tests showed that the 'bone' was not human at all, and that the arrow was probably Inuit, made from caribou antler or walrus ivory.

When the Australian-built replica of the *Endeavour* reached Whitby on its first visit to Britain in 1997 it was greeted by huge crowds. To mark the vessel's emotional 'homecoming' there were flags and bunting, receptions and speeches, guided shipboard tours, and in the gift shop on the quay *Endeavour* sweaters, mugs, postcards and videos – everything except a decent book on Cook's voyages. In town the most readily available book on Cook was the paperback edition of Richard Hough's biography, based on Beaglehole, but ignoring almost all post-Beaglehole scholarship. Dalrymple's work, we read, was 'bogus', Johann Forster was a 'shady bore', and there was no reference to the work of Bernard Smith, Marshall Sahlins and the others. Just as HM Bark *Endeavour* was, of necessity, a safety-first version of the original – with engines, telephone and wireless communication, flush toilets and the rest – so the depiction of Cook had been sanitised for mass consumption.

In many ways things are changing. In the last few years there have been important studies of Cook by Nicholas Thomas, Anne Salmond and John Gascoigne, which represent the best of post-Beaglehole scholarship, as well as more popular books, part biographies, part travelogues, by authors such as Vanessa Collingridge and Tony Horwitz. In Australia and New Zealand Cook's voyages continue to

20. The replica of HM Bark Endeavour, *entering Whitby Harbour, May 1997.*

attract artists, many impelled by a political agenda. Gordon Bennett is the latest Aboriginal artist to paint scenes from the voyages, with paintings such as 'Possession Island' highly valued in the commercial art market; while in New Zealand Michel Tuffery, of Samoan-Tahitian descent, has produced a 'First Contact' series that includes bronze busts called

'Cookies'. At Sydney airport's international terminal opened for the 2000 Olympics a huge wall-mounted sculpture by Fiona McDonald includes scenes of Aboriginal life, accompanied by a line from Cook's judgement on the Aborigines he had seen, fleetingly, in 1770: 'They live in a Tranquillity which is not disturb'd by the Inequality of Condition.' One of the most original contributions within the field of the arts has come from the Maori poet Robert Sullivan, whose book-length poem, 'Captain Cook in the Underworld', was written in 2002 as the libretto for John Psathas's oratorio, *Orpheus in Rarohenga*. This is no simple indictment of the intruder, for Cook is revealed as a man torn by different emotions in which an initial reluctance to kill is overborne by the fact that 'we had *people* on board, mercy was too risky'. In a few ominous words the poet pictures Cook's ship, sailing into the Pacific with

> our leprous cargo of VD
> stashed with lower and higher men, quills
> spilling ink, guns for the kill

Museums around the world have galleries and exhibitions on Cook's voyages that try to represent current views on the relationship between European explorers and indigenous peoples. In the Australian National Maritime Museum in Sydney one display cabinet, labelled 'Captain Cook 1728–1779: Hero or Invader', points out that Cook never sought the 'Consent of the Natives' before claiming possession of the eastern part of the Australian continent, and that his explorations led to the establishment of a convict colony. The 2006 exhibition, 'Life in the Pacific of the 1700s' at the Honolulu Academy of the Arts, juxtaposes Hawaiian objects collected on Cook's voyages with the published journals and the paintings of Hodges and Webber. The tone is set by a large wall map of the Pacific that combines the awe-inspiring tracks of the Polynesian voyagers with Cook's routes across the ocean.

The opening of a new gallery, 'Oceans of Discovery', at the National Maritime Museum, Greenwich, in 2002 was accompanied by a book of essays on Cook that summarised much recent scholarship. That summer the BBC presented multi-episode programmes on Cook's voyages, on radio and on television. The latter series, *The Ship*, was filmed on board the *Endeavour* replica, and was accompanied by a lavishly-illustrated book aimed at a wide readership. The book's opening sentences admitted that Cook has been

> lauded as a founding father of Australia and New Zealand and celebrated as an icon of discovery and exploration … In recent years, however, Cook has become a more ambivalent figure … a symbol of the colonialism, dispossession and oppression that sometimes followed in the wake of his explorations.

This dualism – respect for Cook as a seaman, but misgivings about the implications of his voyages – is now a familiar theme among a whole range of reactions to the explorer. Sailing on the *Endeavour* during the shooting of the television series were – unhistorically – three Maori and three Aborigines. One of the latter, Bruce Gibson, head of the Injinoo Land Trust at Cape York, derided the comfortable view of the replica as

> a means of learning that provides a bridge to

understanding between cultures ... The *Endeavour* is a proud symbol for white Australia, but for most Aborigines it is an insulting thing ... a painful reminder of our tragic history as well as our present, languishing condition as a people in modern Australia.

It is in Australia that opinion about Cook is most sharply divided on racial lines. Aboriginal histories, songs and paintings from parts of the continent stretching from Botany Bay to the Kimberley region in northwest Australia identify 'Captain Cook' as the emblematic invader, the despoiler of their lands over wide expanses of space and time. As Tommy Vincent Lingiyarri put it:

A thousand million years ago
Before I was born
Captain Cook sailed out from big England
And started shooting all my people

In truth, Cook in his original journal made such a determined attempt to extol the Aboriginal lifestyle that his comments were (unusually) criticised by Beaglehole as 'nonsense'; but as a more recent scholar has explained, for many of today's Aborigines Cook is forever 'the persona of conquest'. Some draw a distinction between Cook, whose generally humane record they recognise, and his more violent successors. So Paddy Fordham Wainburranga in Central Arnhem Land asserted that, 'C.C. wasn't a bad man.' But, 'When the old C.C. died, other people started thinking they could make C.C. another way. New people. Maybe all his sons. Too many Captain Cooks.' If any single individual from Cook's voyages should be held responsible for the dispatch of the First Fleet to

Australia and all that followed then it was Joseph Banks, with his persuasive depiction of Botany Bay, and his insistence that its few native inhabitants could be ignored; but a uniformed figure makes a more obvious adversary. So, the painting by the Aboriginal artist, H.J. Wedge, 'Captain Cook Con Man', has Cook dressed in military red and brandishing a sword, with an explanation that it 'shows Captain Cook standing so proud that he has stolen a new land for the British Empire'.

In Hawai'i, nationalist activists now deride the 'Western' representation of Cook taught to them as children. As Haunani-Kay Trask remembers, 'At school I learned that the "pagan Hawaiians" did not read or write, were lustful cannibals ... Captain Cook had "discovered" Hawai'i, and the ungrateful Hawaians had killed him.' Rather, they dwell on his identity as the destroyer of their ancient culture, though few carry their anger as far as Lilikal'a Kame'eleihiwa who describes how she taught her students that

> the best part of Cook's visit was that we killed him ... in our dealings with those admirably fierce Maori ... we can defend our honour by declaring that we rid the world of another evil white man.

That not all Hawaiians think this way can be seen in the popular enthusiasm that greeted the first visit of the *Endeavour* replica to the islands in 1999. Local newspapers extolled its merits as a tourist and educational attraction, and the main threat to the vessel came from accidental encounters with the concrete piers of Kona and Honolulu.

In Western Canada, a region not often associated with Cook, Native (First Nations) oral traditions recount Cook's arrival on their shores. The difference between these recollections and the older Canadian textbook celebration of Cook's month at Nootka Sound is abrupt. In the latter, Cook's stay on the shores of what was to become British Columbia opened the way, first to maritime fur traders, and then to settlers and the benefits of British rule. As a local newspaper explained at the time of the unveiling of a cairn at Nootka Sound in 1924, the place was 'perhaps the most historic site of all in British Columbia'. A Yuquot fisherman in the Sound recollects the story of Cook's arrival in a less flattering way:

> Captain Cook, he was out there lost in the fog when [chief] Maquinna's great-grandfather took a bunch of warriors and guided his ship in. The people then helped nurse the crew back to health. They were in poor shape. They stayed across in Resolution Sound for over a month, repairing their ship. During that time Captain Cook and his crew used to go to Yuquot Cove, treat the ladies in a real mean way, and raid whatever they could get their hands on: smokehouses and sundried fish. Then they left for Hawaii or somewhere.

In recent years the early contacts between the Native peoples of British Columbia and white explorers and traders have taken on an important legal dimension as the courts are called upon to decide land issues, and weigh the evidence of Native oral traditions against the written records of the new arrivals. In one of the most controversial of these decisions the Chief Justice pronounced that the Native witnesses had 'a romantic view of their history', an observation that could equally be applied to the editorial manipulations of the journals of Cook and his successors.

As the story of Cook and his voyages is told and retold,

George Forster's words come to mind: 'What Cook has added to our store of knowledge is so constituted that it will grow deep roots and long have a decisive influence on the activities of mankind.' Reassessments of Cook tend to follow two tracks. First, there is a reappraisal of him as an explorer, and here today's Cook is not Douglas's, or even Beaglehole's. He is set more firmly in a context of collaboration and mutual help both on shipboard and in England, while there has been a sharpening of Beaglehole's worry about Cook's erratic behaviour on the third voyage. That said, there is not any significant diminution of regard for Cook's achievements as an explorer. He was, as Sandwich said after his second voyage, 'the first navigator in Europe', the man who transformed the map of the world with a minimum loss of life to his own crews or to the peoples of the Pacific. This probably still represents the thinking of most people for whom the name of Captain Cook means something.

What is altogether more open to debate is Cook's role as a force in Europe's entry into the Pacific, its invasion as some, probably a minority, would regard it. How far should an explorer following official instructions be held responsible for the long-term consequences of his actions? This is not an altogether straightforward issue. When in a ceremony on Possession Island in August 1770 on his first voyage Cook claimed the east coast of Australia for the British crown, he was both following his instructions and exceeding them. His sailing orders in 1768 had given him instructions that he was

with the Consent of the Natives to take possession of Convenient Situations in the Country in the Name of the King of Great Britain; or, if you find the Country uninhabited, take Possession … as first discoverers and possessors.

Cook's decision in early 1770 to head towards, and survey, the unknown coast was his own, as was his subsequent decision to take possession without 'the Consent of the Natives' of a region parts of which were clearly peopled, although the inhabitants seemed to be few in number and without recognisable political organisation. The personal nature of the double decision is a reminder that it would be as wrong to regard Cook as an unwitting agent of British imperialism as to fall into the trap of blaming him for what happened afterwards. He was more sensitive than most to the likely repercussions of the European arrival in the Pacific; but his command of successive voyages indicated both his professional commitment and his patriotic belief that if a European nation should dominate the lands and waters of the Pacific then it should be Britain.

FURTHER READING

For printed books, the place of publication is London unless otherwise stated.

GENERAL

Modern Cook scholarship has its foundation in the superb annotated editions by J. C. Beaglehole of the explorer's manuscript journals, published by the Hakluyt Society: *The Journals of Captain James Cook*: I, *The Voyage of the* Endeavour *1768–1771* (Cambridge, 1955); II, *The Voyage of the* Resolution *and* Adventure *1772–1776* (Cambridge, 1961); III, *The Voyage of the* Resolution *and* Discovery *1776–1780* (2 vols, Cambridge, 1967) cited hereafter as Beaglehole, I, II, III. They include not only Cook's journals, but extracts from the journals of other officers and crew members, as well as correspondence from Cook and others. An abridged version of Beaglehole's volumes is Philip Edwards, (ed.), *The Journals of Captain Cook* (Harmondsworth, 1999). These texts can be supplemented by Rüddiger Joppien and Bernard Smith, (eds), *The Art of Captain Cook's Voyages* (3 vols, New Haven and London, 1985–1988), and Andrew David, (ed.), *The Charts and Coastal Views of Captain Cook's Voyages* (1988–1997). Useful reference works edited by John Robson are *Captain Cook's World:*

Maps of the Life and Voyages of James Cook R. N. (Auckland, 2000) and *The Captain Cook Encyclopaedia* (2004). The standard biography of Cook remains J. C. Beaglehole, *The Life of Captain James Cook* (1974). Outstanding among recent books on Cook's Pacific voyages are Anne Salmond, *The Trial of the Cannibal Dog: Captain Cook in the South Seas* (2003); Nicholas Thomas, *Discoveries: The Voyages of Captain Cook* (2003); and John Gascoigne, *Captain Cook: Voyager Between Worlds* (2007). Among many websites dealing with Cook's voyages are:

http:southseas.nla.gov.au

http:pages.quicksilver.net.nz/jcr/~cooky.html

http://www.CaptainCookSociety.com

CHAPTER 1 A DISTANT DEATH

Gore's 'gingerbread' letter and Cook's letter to Sandwich are in Beaglehole, III, pp. 1522, 1520. The February 1776 dinner party is described in Andrew Kippis, *The Life of Captain James Cook* (1788), pp. 324–5. Cook's letters to Walker are in Beaglehole, II, p. 960 and Beaglehole, III, p. 1488. Retirement ages on Whitby ships are tabulated in Rosalin Barker, 'Cook's Nursery: Whitby's eighteenth-century merchant fleet', in Glyn Williams, *Captain Cook: Explorations and Reassessments* (Woodbridge, Suffolk, 2004), pp. 7–20. Lists of floggings on Cook's voyages are given in Salmond, *Trial of the Cannibal Dog*, pp. 433–7. Cook's last letter and those from Clerke, Harris and Banks are in Beaglehole, III, pp. 1530–32, 1535–40, 1547–8, 1552–3, 1553–4, while Pallas's letter to Pennant is printed in C. M. Hotimsky, *The Death of Captain James Cook: A Letter from Russia in 1779* (Sydney, 1962). The Royal Society's commemorative medal is described in L. Richard Smith, *The Royal Society Cook Medal* (Sydney, 1982), and in Andrew

S. Cook, 'James Cook and the Royal Society', in Williams, *Captain Cook*, pp. 37–55.

Gilbert's 'tedious' voyage complaint is in Christine Holmes, *Captain Cook's Final Voyage: The Journal of Midshipman George Gilbert* (Horsham, 1982), p. 157. For Bligh's 'threats of printing' see Beaglehole, III, p. ccv. The unofficial accounts of the voyage are John Rickman, *Journal of Captain Cook's Last Voyage to the Pacific Ocean* (1781); Heinrich Zimmermann, trs. F. W. Howay, *Zimmermann's Captain Cook* (Mannheim, 1781, Toronto, 1930); William Ellis, *An authentic Narrative of a Voyage performed by Captain Cook and Captain Clerke* (2 vols, 1782); John Ledyard, *A Journal of Captain's Cook's last Voyage to the Pacific Ocean* (Hartford, Conn., 1783); David Samwell, *A Narrative of the Death of Captain James Cook* (1786; also published in Martin Fitzpatrick, Nicholas Thomas and Jennifer Newell, *The Death of Captain Cook*, Cardiff, 2007). Polynesian canoe-building is described in Paul D'Arcy, *The People of the Sea: Environment, Identity and History in Oceania* (Honolulu, 2006), pp. 90–93.

Horace Walpole's comment on Cook's published journal is quoted in Daniel Clayton, *Islands of Truth: The Imperial Fashioning of Vancouver Island* (Vancouver, 2000), p. 245n.5.

One of the best accounts of the events at Kealakekua Bay remains Gavin Kennedy, *The Death of Captain Cook* (1978). Reports about Kalani'opu'u's dissatisfaction at the return of the ships are in Beaglehole, III, p. 528n., and in Marshall Sahlins, *How 'Natives' Think About Captain Cook, For Example* (Chicago and London, 1995), pp. 80–1. Williamson's comments on ball versus small-shot are in Beaglehole, III, pp. 1348–9. References to the iron dagger are in J. R. Forster, *History of the Voyages and Discoveries made in the North* (1786), p. 404, and Beaglehole, III, p. 538. For Thomas's comments on the death of Cook see *Discoveries*, p. 394, and Fitzpatrick et al., *Death of Cook by Samwell*, p. 51. Individual crew narratives of Cook's death are scrutinised in O. H. K. Spate, 'Splicing the Log at Kealakekua Bay: James King's Sleight of Hand', *Journal of Pacific History*, 19 (1984), pp. 117–20; Kerry Howe, 'The Death of Cook: Exercises in Explanation' in Jonathan Lamb, (ed.), *The South Pacific in the Eighteenth Century: Narratives and Myths* (*Eighteenth-Century Life*, vol 18, 1994), pp. 198–211; and Scott Ashley, 'How navigators think: "The Death of Captain Cook Revisited"', *Past and Present*, no. 194 (2007), pp. 107–37. Details of Phillips's lost journal are in Beaglehole, III, p. clxxvi*n*. Gilbert's reference to the impact of Cook's death on the crew of the *Resolution* is in Holmes, *Captain Cook's Final Voyage*, p.107; Edgar's description of the burial ceremony in Beaglehole, III, p. 548*n*.

The various versions of Cook's journal and log referred to here are in the British Library: Egerton MSS 2177A (holograph journal), 2177B (log fragment), 2179, 2189 (Douglas's edited copy), and The National Archives: Adm 55/111–13 (clerical copy of the journal). Douglas's comments on his editing of Cook's journal are in Cook and King, *Voyage to the Pacific Ocean*, I, p. lxxvii (and Beaglehole, III, p. cxcix). Douglas's changes made to Cook's journal entries covering the stay at Nootka Sound are dissected in I.S. MacLaren, 'Exploration/Travel Literature and the Evolution of the Author', *International Journal of Canadian Studies*, 5 (1992), pp. 39–68, and Noel Elizabeth Currie, *Constructing Colonial Discourse: Captain Cook at Nootka Sound* (Montreal and Kingston, 2005). For the problems of naval stores and of Williamson's behaviour see Beaglehole, III, pp. 482*n*. and 536*n*. – 537*n*. Captain Thompson's comment on Williamson is in his diary entry for 27 November 1784 in the British Library: Add MS 46,120, fo.32r. The authorship claims of Dampier, Rogers and Cook are set out in William Dampier, *A Voyage to New-Holland &c. In the Year 1699* (1703), preface; Woodes Rogers, *A Cruising Voyage Round the World* (1712), p. 1; James Cook, *A Voyage towards the South Pole, and Round the World* (2 vols,1777), I, p. xxxvi. Philip Edwards' comments are in *The story of the voyage: sea-narratives in eighteenth-century England* (Cambridge, 1994), p. 10.

Correspondence and other evidence about Cook's papers are in Beaglehole, III, pp. clxxi–v. Suspicions about Cook's missing journal are aired in Salmond, *Trial of the Cannibal Dog*, p. 420 and Gananath Obeyesekere, *The Apotheosis of Captain Cook: European Mythmaking in the Pacific* (2nd edn, Princeton, 1992), p. 274n.29. The possible destruction of Clerke's notes on the Williamson affair is mentioned in Fitzpatrick et al., *Death of Cook by Samwell*, p. 77. Cook's concern about the tone of his second voyage account is in Beaglehole, II, p. cxlvi. The claim that Cook's journal was complete up until his death is made in *Monthly Review*, vol. 67, June 1782, p. 68. Evidence that Cook material was kept by the Douglas family is in Beaglehole, III, p. clxxii.

CHAPTER 2 AN ENLIGHTENMENT HERO

Furneaux's report of 5 April 1774 is in The National Archives: Adm 1/1789. The report of Cook's farthest south is in *Lloyd's Evening Post*, 7–9 August 1775. Pringle's address of 30 November 1776 to the Royal Society was printed in James Cook, *A Voyage towards the South Pole, and Round the World* (1777), pp. 369–96. The *Gentleman's Magazine* comments on Cook's second voyage are in vol. XLVII (1777), pp. 179, 493. The newspaper and periodical entries on Cook's death are in the *Morning Chronicle*, 14 and 22 January 1780 and in the *Gentleman's Magazine*, vol. L (1780), p. 44. The eulogy to Cook in the authorised account is in Cook and King, *Voyage to the North Pacific Ocean*, I, pp. lxxxvii–ix; Zimmermann's tribute is in Howay, *Zimmermann's Captain Cook*, p. 102. 'The ocean may be his grave' quotation is from Anon., *Remarks and Conjectures on the Voyage of the Ships* Resolution *and* Discovery (London, 1780), p. 44. The French and American orders to respect Cook's ships are in Beaglehole, III, pp. 1535, 1542, 1556, 1557. For the Spanish attitude to Cook see Christon I. Archer, 'The Spanish Reaction to Cook's Third Voyage', in Robin Fisher and Hugh Johnston (eds), *Captain James Cook and His Times* (Vancouver, 1979), pp. 105–6. The French diplomat's request is in The National Archives: Adm FP/25, 4 June 1782. On the French elegies of Cook see William Scott, 'Cook, France and the Savages', in Paul Dukes, (ed.), *Frontiers of European Culture* (Lampeter, 1996), pp. 171–92.

Bernard Smith, 'Cook's Posthumous Reputation', in his *Imagining the Pacific: In the Wake of the Cook Voyages* (New Haven and London, 1992), pp. 225–40 is a key essay, and includes a discussion of paintings of the death of Cook. For a more recent discussion on 'Captain Cook and English Ethnicity' see Kathleen Wilson, *The Island Race: Englishness, empire and gender in the eighteenth century* (2003), ch. 2. Webber's note on the engraving of the death of Cook is reproduced in *Hordern House: The Parsons Collection Part I Dampier to Cook* (Sydney, 2006), item 137. The remarks on Cook by Grillparzer and Goethe are in Leslie Bodi, 'Captain Cook in German Imaginative Literature', in Walter Veit, (ed.), *Captain James Cook: Image and Impact* (Melbourne, 1972), pp. 128–9, 132. Benjamin West's comments are quoted in Nicholas Tracy, *Britannia's Palette: The Arts of Naval Victory* (Montreal and Kingston, 2007), p. 174. Reproductions, with comments, of the recently-discovered watercolours by John Cleveley are in Christie's catalogue, 'Exploration and Travel with The Polar Sale', 22 September 2004, pp. 44–60. The pantomime *Omai* is discussed, with illustrations, in Rüddiger Joppien, 'Philippe Jacques de Loutherbourg's Pantomime "Omai, or a Trip round the World" and the Artists of Captain Cook's Voyages', in T. C. Mitchell, (ed.), *Captain Cook and the South Pacific* (1979), pp. 81–136, and in David Worrall, *Harlequin Empire: Race, Ethnicity and the Drama of the Popular Enlightenment* (2007), ch. 6. The contents of the Sandwich Room in the Leverian Museum are described in *A Companion to the Museum, (Late Sir Ashton Lever's)* (1790), pp. 6–25. Thompson's comparison of Cook and Clerke is in his diary for 29 December 1784 in British Library: Add MS 46120, fo.43v; Samwell's explanation for writing his *Narrative* is in the book's preface. The quotations from Arthur Kippis are in his *Life of Captain James Cook* (1788), II, pp. 298, 299, 300–1. The criticism of Kippis in the *Gentleman's Magazine* is in vol. LVIII (1788), p.617; of Hawkesworth in vol. XLV (1775), p. 132. For the comments of George Forster, Horace Walpole and James Dunbar see Nicholas Thomas and Oliver Berghof, (eds), *George Forster: A Voyage Round the World* (Honolulu, 2000), I, p. 200; W. S. Lewis, (ed.), *The Yale Edition of Horace Walpole's Correspondence*, II (New Haven, 1937), p. 225; James Dunbar, *Essays on the History of Mankind* (1780), pp. 356–7. Cook's comment at Queen Charlotte Sound is in Beaglehole, *Journals*, II, p. 175. The unconventional reaction to the news of Cook's death is in *Morning Chronicle*, 17 January 1780; the *Critical Review* on the authorised account of Cook's last voyage is in vol. 58 (1784), *passim*.

George Forster's essay 'Cook, der Entdecker' is now

available in English translation in *Cook, the Discoverer by George Forster* (Sydney, 2007). See also Michael Hoare, '"Cook the Discoverer": an essay by George Forster, 1787', *Records of the Australian Academy of Science*, I (1969), pp. 7–16. The Boswell comment is quoted in Beaglehole, *Life of Cook*, p. 451. The relationship between Cook and Gore is examined in Salmond, *Trial of the Cannibal Dog*, pp. 130–1. Zimmermann's description of Cook is in Howay, *Zimmermann's Captain Cook*, pp. 98–100, and Trevenen's on Cook's *heiva* in Beaglehole, III, p. cliii. The troubles of Dampier and Rogers are examined in Glyn Williams, *The Great South Sea: English Voyages and Encounters 1570–1750* (1997), ch. V. William Barr, *Arctic Hell-Ship: the Voyage of HMS Enterprise 1850–1855* (Edmonton, 2007) has descriptions of tensions on one Arctic expedition that make those on Cook's voyages appear trivial. The aftermath of Cook's voyages is covered in David Mackay, *In the Wake of Cook: Exploration, Science & Empire 1780–1801* (1985), and in Alan Frost, *The Global Reach of Empire: Britain's maritime expansion in the Indian and Pacific oceans 1764–1815* (Melbourne, 2003). Dalrymple's comment on Cook is in The National Archives: C.0.42/72, p. 501.

For Cook and the French royal family see Smith, *European Vision*, p. 137. The remarks of La Pérouse and D'Urville on Cook are in John Dunmore, (ed.), *The Journal of Jean François de Galaup de la Pérouse 1785–1788* (1994), I, p. 78, and J. S. C. Dumont d'Urville, *Voyage au Pôle Sud* (Paris, 1841), I, p. lxiv. For Malaspina see John Kendrick, *Alejandro Malaspina: Portrait of a Visionary* (Montreal and Kingston, 1999). Russian attitudes to Cook are examined in Yakov M. Svet and Svetlana G. Fedorova, 'Captain Cook and the Russians', *Pacific Studies*, II (1978), pp. 1–9; Terence Armstrong, 'Cook's Reputation in Russia', in Fisher and Johnston, *Captain Cook and*

His Times, pp. 121–8; and Simon Werrett, 'Russian responses to the voyages of Captain Cook', in Williams, *Captain Cook*, pp. 179–97. For the reactions of individual Russian explorers see Otto von Kotzebue, *A Voyage of Discovery into the South Sea* (1821), I, p. 3; Adelbert von Chamisso, *A Voyage round the World ... 1815–1818* (Honolulu, 1986), p. 8; V. M. Golovin, *Around the World ... 1817–1819*, trs. Ella L.Wiswell (Honolulu, 1979), p. 179.

Nathaniel Portlock's visit to Hawai'i is described in his *Voyage Round the World but more particularly to the North-West Coast of America* (1789), especially pp. 61, 309. For La Pérouse at Maui see Dunmore, *Journal of La Pérouse*, I, p. 85. Details of the visits to Hawai'i by Meares and Douglas are in John Meares, *Voyages from China to the North West Coast of America* (1790), pp. 4–10, 13–15, 343–4; of Colnett's visit to Kauai in Robert Galois, (ed.), *A Voyage to the North West Side of America: The Journals of James Colnett, 1786–89* (Vancouver and Toronto, 2004), pp. 188, 192, 388–9, and in John Nicol, *Life and Adventures 1776–1801*, Tim Flannery, (ed.) (Melbourne, 1997), p. 83. The differing views on the identity of Cook's killer are in Beaglehole, III, p. 557*n*. (Trevenen), ibid., p. 1202 (Samwell in 1779), and Fitzpatrick et al., *Death of Cook by Samwell*, p. 78 (Samwell in 1786). Vancouver's comments during his visits to Hawai'i are in W. Kaye Lamb, (ed.), *A Voyage of Discovery to the North Pacific Ocean* (1984), I, p. 71, III, pp. 811, 821–2, 1164. Bell's remarks on the death of Cook are in Obeyeskere, *Apotheosis of Captain Cook*, pp. 151, 186; Puget's in British Library: Add MS 17,548, fo.2; Dimsdell's in Beaglehole, III, p. 557*n*.3; Mariner's in John Martin, *An Account of the Natives of the Tonga Islands* (Edinburgh, 1827), II, p. 67; Little's in George Little, *Life on the Ocean* (Boston, 12th edn, 1846), pp. 131–2. For Byron's official visit see Robert Dampier, *To the*

Sandwich Islands in H.M.S. Blonde, Pauline King Joerger, (ed.) (Honolulu, 1971), pp. 65–7, 70. A. L. Korn, *The Victorian Visitors* (Honolulu, 1958), p. 65 describes Lady Franklin's visit to Kealakekua Bay; extracts from Mark Twain's account, introduced by Vanessa Smith, are in Lamb et al., *Exploration and Exchange*, pp. 275–91.

For Cook at Nootka Sound see Daniel Clayton, *Islands of Truth: The Imperial Fashioning of Vancouver Island* (Vancouver and Toronto, 2000), pp. 23–7 and Robin Fisher, 'Cook and the Nootka' in Fisher and Johnston, *Captain James Cook and His Times*, pp. 81–98. Elliott's description is in Beaglehole, *Journals*, II, p. 124*n*.3. For 'Cookees', Rickman's comment, Cook as 'Tute', and later Hawai'ian accounts see Salmond, *Trial of the Cannibal Dog*, pp. 490*n*.17, 401–2, 392–3, 380, 383. Bridget Orr, '"Southern Passions mix with northern art": Miscegenation and the *Endeavour* Voyage', and Lee Wallace, 'Too Darn Hot: Sexual Contact in the Sandwich Islands on Cook's Third Voyage', in Lamb, *South Pacific in the Eighteenth Century*, pp. 212–31 and 232–42, discuss Cook's sexual abstinence. Puget, Dimsdell and Colnett are quoted in Sahlins, *How "Natives" Think*, pp. 95–7, 92. Cook's misadventures on Tonga are discussed in Salmond, *Trial of the Cannibal Dog*, p. 348, and Martin, *Account of the Natives of the Tonga Islands*, II, pp. 71–2. For Maori memories of Cook see Anne Salmond, *Two Worlds: First Meetings between Maori and Europeans 1642–1772* (Auckland, 1991), pp. 87–8, 123–4, 206–7 and *Between Worlds: Early Exchanges Between Maori and Europeans* (Honolulu, 1997), pp. 126–7. For recent research on Tupa'ia see Glyn Williams, 'Tupa'ia: Polynesian warrior, navigator, high priest – and artist', in Felicity A. Nussbaum, (ed.), *The Global Eighteenth Century* (Baltimore and London, 2003), pp. 38–51. For the contradictory messages at Tahiti about Cook's death see Gavin Kennedy, *Captain Bligh: the man and his mutinies* (1989), p. 46 and Paul G. Fidlon and R. J. Ryan, (eds), *The Journal of Arthur Bowes Smyth: Surgeon*, Lady Penrhyn *1787–1789* (Sydney, 1979), p. 99. The story of Cook's portrait at Tahiti is told in Greg Dening, *Mr Bligh's Bad Language: Passion, Power and Theatre on the Bounty* (Cambridge, 1992), pp. 207–8; James Morrison, *The Journal of James Morrison, Boatswain's mate of the Bounty* (1935), p. 85; George Hamilton, *A Voyage Round the World In His Majesty's Frigate Pandora* (repr. Sydney, 1998), pp. 57, 59. For memories of Cook in the Marquesas, see Greg Dening, *Beach Crossings: Voyaging across times, cultures and self* (Carlton, Victoria, 2004), p. 235; in Tahiti, Rod Edmond, *Representing the South Pacific: Colonial Discourse from Cook to Gauguin* (Cambridge, 1997), p. 46; in the Gilbert Islands, Robert Louis Stevenson, *In the South Seas* (Edinburgh, 1896, ed. Neil Rennie, 1998), p. 234.

CHAPTER 3 COOK IN THE COLONIAL AGE

Bernard Smith's 'hero' note is in Fisher and Johnston, *Captain James Cook and His Times*, p. 168. For Cook monuments see Cliff Thornton, *Captain Cook in Cleveland* (Stroud, 2006), ch. XI; and Kippis, *Life of Cook*, II, p. 316. Extracts from Haweis's sermon are quoted in Smith, *European Vision*, p. 144. The Dickens references are in Edmond, *Representing the South Pacific*, p. 42. William Ellis describes his visit to Kealakekua Bay in *Narrative of a Tour Through Hawaii* (1826). Comparisons between Cook and John Williams are made by Sujit Sivasundaram in 'Redeeming Memory: the martyrdoms of Captain James Cook and Reverend John Williams', in Williams, *Captain Cook*, pp. 201–29.

For commemorations of Cook in nineteenth-century

Australia see Christopher Healy, *From the Ruins of Colonialism* (Cambridge, 1997), pp. 21–9 and Jillian Robertson, *The Captain Cook Myth* (Sydney, 1981), pp. 110–26. The 1901 re-enactment at Botany Bay is described in 'The Landing of James Cook' [1901], copy in British Library 11781 a.50. Cook's reputation in New Zealand is discussed in David Mackay, 'Exploring the Pacific, Exploring James Cook', in Frost and Samson, *Pacific Empires*, pp. 251–69.

The fluctuating reputation of Cook in Hawai'i can be followed in Ellis, *Narrative* and in his *Polynesian Researches* (1829); Sheldon Dibble, *History of the Sandwich Islands* (Lahainaluna, 1843); David Malo, *Hawaiian Antiquities* (Honolulu, 1903); Samuel M. Kamakau, *Ka Po'e Kahiko: The People of Old* (Honolulu, 1962); James J. Jarves, *History of the Hawaiian or Sandwich Islands* (Boston, 1843); Hiram Bingham, *A Residence of Twenty-One Years in the Sandwich Islands* (Hartford, 1848); John F. G. Stokes, *Origin of the Condemnation of Captain Cook in Hawaii* (Honolulu, 1930). The 1928 commemoration of Cook's visit is described in A.P. Taylor, *Sesquicentennial Celebration of Captain Cook's Discovery of Hawaii* (Honolulu, 1929) and Joseph Carruthers, *Captain James Cook, R. N. One hundred and fifty years after* (1930).

CHAPTER 4 COOK IN A POSTCOLONIAL WORLD

For comments on Beaglehole's biography of Cook see Fisher and Johnston, *Captain James Cook and His Times*, p. 2; followed by Michael Hoare's analysis on pp. 213–24. More detail on Beaglehole's work on Cook is in Tim Beaglehole, *A Life of J. C. Beaglehole: New Zealand Scholar* (Wellington, 2006). Smith's analysis of Cook's voyages is in *European Vision*, p. 51; Moorehead's in *Fatal Impact: An Account of the Invasion of the South Pacific 1767–1840* (Harmondsworth, 1968), pp. 14, 19. The criticism of Smith's essays was made by Jeanette Horn in *The Age*, 10 October 1992. For the service at Anaura Bay see the *New Zealand Herald*, 19 January 1996.

Gavan Daws' interpretation of the death of Cook was first advanced in 'Kealakekua Bay revisited: a note on the death of Captain Cook', *Journal of Pacific History*, 3 (1968), pp. 21–3, and then expanded in his *Shoal of Time: A History of the Hawaiian Islands* (Honolulu, 1968), pp. 1–29. J. C. Beaglehole's lecture, *The Death of Captain Cook* (Wellington, 1979) sums up much of his thinking on the subject. For the debate between Sahlins and Obeyesekere see Marshall Sahlins, *Islands of History* (Chicago, 1985) and *How "Natives" Think*; and Obeyesekere, *Apotheosis of Captain Cook*. A perceptive summary of the debate is in Edmond, 'Killing the god: the afterlife of Cook's death', in *Representing the South Pacific*, pp. 23–62. See also Oskar Spate, *Paradise Found and Lost* (Canberra, 1988), p. 145; Greg Dening, *Performances* (Melbourne, 1996), p. 77.

Examples of Cook's reputation today are in notes in *Cook's Log* by Cliff Thornton, vol. 27, no. 3 (2004), Daphne Salt, vol. 28, no. 1 (2005), and Fred Mckinnon, vol. 29, no. 2 (2006). There are extensive descriptions and photographs of locations associated with Cook in Mark Adams and Nicholas Thomas, *Cook's Sites: Revisiting History* (Otago, 1999) and in Nicholas Thomas, 'The Uses of Captain Cook: early exploration in the public history of Aotearoa New Zealand and Australia', in Annie Coombes, (ed.), *Rethinking Settler Colonialism: History and Memory*, ch. 7 (Manchester, 2006). The televised voyage of the *Endeavour* replica is described in Simon Baker, *The Ship: Retracing Cook's Endeavour Voyage* (2002), pp. 6, 12, 139–40. For Aboriginal reactions to Cook see

Chris Healy, 'Captain Cook: Between White and Black', and Paddy Fordham Wainburranga, 'Too many Captain Cooks', in Sylvia Kleinhert and Margo Neale, (eds), *The Oxford Companion to Aboriginal Art and Culture* (Melbourne, 2000), pp. 92–6; Deborah Bird Rose, *Dingo Makes Us Human* (Cambridge, 1992), pp. 44, 187–9; H. J. Wedge, *Wiradjuri Spirit Man* (Roseville East, NSW, 1996), pp. 12, 46. Haunani-Kay Trask describes Hawaiian schoolday recollections of Cook in *From a Native Daughter* (Monroe, Maine, 1993), p. 7; for 'we rid the world of another evil white man' see the review by Lilikal'a Kame'eleihiwa of Obeyesekere, *Apotheosis of Captain Cook*, in *Pacific Studies*, 17 (1994), pp. 111–18. The Yuquot man's description of Cook's arrival at Nootka Sound is quoted in Currie, *Constructing Colonial Discourse*, p. 148; see also Clayton, *Islands of Truth*. George Forster's prophecy is in his *Cook, the Discoverer*, p. 259.

LIST OF ILLUSTRATIONS

ILLUSTRATION CREDITS

1, National Portrait Gallery, London; 2, State Library of New South Wales; 3, Alan Frost; 4, 5, 6, 8, 15, 16, endpapers, Captain Cook Memorial Museum, Whitby; 7, British Library; 9, 10, 11, 14, 18, National Library of Australia; 12, 13, Christie's Images Ltd; 17, Sophie Forgan; 19, Yuri Dunaev; 20, *Whitby Gazette*

ACKNOWLEDGEMENTS

During the writing of this book, I have been helped by scholars from many parts of the world. Tim Beaglehole, Sophie
Forgan, Alan Frost, Robin Inglis and David Mackay are
among those who have accompanied (or taken) me to locations associated with Captain Cook, from Great Ayton in
Yorkshire to Ship Cove in New Zealand, from Kealakekua
Bay in Hawai'i to Nootka Sound on Vancouver Island. Ian
Boreham, Andrew Cook, Pat Crimmin, Andrew David,
Jonathan Lamb, Doug Munro, Bridget Orr, Geoff Quilley,
and the late Fritz Rehbock, have helped with information
and advice. Anne Salmond and Nicholas Thomas have performed the tedious but (for the author) immensely useful
task of reading parts of the text in draft. At Profile Books
Peter Carson and Nicola Taplin have been marvellously sup-
portive, while a flow of e-mail suggestions from Mary Beard
is evidence of her meticulous care as series editor. It remains
to be said that the book could not have been written without
the help of those publications listed under Further Reading.
It is a privilege to feel that I belong to the community of
'Cook scholars' whose work is represented there.

INDEX

PROFILES IN HISTORY

The *Profiles in History* series will explore iconic events and relationships in history. Each book will start from the historical moment: what happened? But each will focus too on the fascinating and often surprising afterlife of the story concerned.

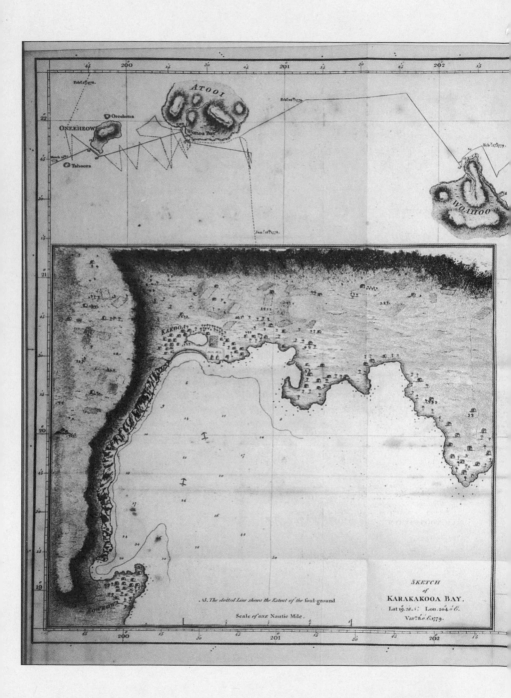

S. The dotted Line shews the Extent of the Foul ground.

Scale of ONE *Nautic Mile.*

SKETCH
of
KARAKAKOOA BAY.
Lat 19. 28. ... Lon. 204. 6 C.
Var.? 10. 6. 1779.